The Church of England Observed

The
Church of England
Observed

RUPERT E. DAVIES

SCM PRESS LTD

334 00229 X

First published 1984 by
SCM Press Ltd
26–30 Tottenham Road London N1 4BZ

Typeset by Gloucester Typesetting Services
and printed in Great Britain by
Richard Clay (The Chaucer Press) Ltd
Bungay, Suffolk

*PRO UNA SANCTA
CATHOLICA ET APOSTOLICA
ECCLESIA*

Contents

Preface

I have written this book out of love for the Church of England. I am a Methodist, and over many decades I have worked with many others to end the separation of Methodists and Anglicans which should never have happened in the first place. In that endeavour I have been brought into close contact with the Church of England, and with its leaders and members, at nearly every level, parochial, civic, diocesan and national; and I have made many friends in that church who share with me my deepest convictions and most constant purposes.

Is the Church of England as ramshackle and confused as its critics make out? No. Is it the finely-tuned instrument of divine grace that its supporters sometimes claim it to be? No. Perhaps a sympathetic observer from just outside can throw light on the truth that must lie between the two extremes.

People speak of 'the dear old Church of England' in tones of affectionate resignation, as if it were a venerable but flawed institution about which nothing can be done. But this is scarcely the image that any serious Anglican wishes to be presented to the world. I have tried to show that this image can be replaced by a quite different one, that of a great church which can lead the Christians of England into unity.

I should like this book to be read not only by clergymen and theological students, though certainly by them, but also by the laypeople, both men and women, without whose massive, well-informed and critical co-operation their church cannot be reformed. And I hope also that it will be read by Free Church people who still cherish the hope of visible unity; for the Church of England, on its own showing, and on mine, is the business of every English Christian.

I acknowledge with thanks great encouragement from the Bishop of Bristol and many other Anglicans, none of whom knew what the contents of the book would be. I am especially grateful to Mrs Mary Tanner, Theological Secretary of the Board for Mission and Unity of the General Synod, and Canon Jim Free, of Bristol Cathedral, who by their careful reading have tried hard to save me from factual errors, but are of course not responsible for my judgments; and to my wife, Margaret, who has shared with me much Anglican friendship and hospitality and a great number of Anglican-Methodist relationships. Mrs Ann Weeks, of Exeter, has once again achieved the impossible task of reading what I have written and typing it out.

Bishopsworth, Bristol   Rupert E. Davies
February 1984

I

The Credentials of the
Church of England

To most English people the right of the Church of England to exist in its present form is not in doubt, any more than is that of the Monarchy or the Constitution. This majority includes most practising Anglicans, as one might expect, though not by any means all those who are critical by temperament or training. It also includes virtually all nominal Anglicans, who have certain expectations of the church, and do not wish it to be disturbed, in case by any chance they should need its services. It includes also a large sector of the population as a whole, who may never enter the parish church except involuntarily, but wish it to be available, just as it is, for family occasions with a vaguely religious significance, and dimly think of it as one of the things which hold society together. It includes, even, many of those who strongly disapprove of what the Church of England believes and does, but wish it to be preserved as a target for their objections to Christianity, and are not above using it for purposes of a social or national nature, when it is convenient to do so.

But there is a considerable minority which does not take the present form and status of the Church of England for granted. Apart from critical Anglicans, it is made up of Christians who belong to the non-Anglican denominations, large and small.

Among them the Roman Catholics form the largest group. In the past they have claimed that the Church of England has usurped the position and buildings of their own church, and they have endured persecution for that belief. Even today their own church, world-wide and calling itself the Catholic Church, still stands over against the Church of England as a kind of not unfriendly rival.

Each of the various Free Churches has its own history in relation to the Church of England. The older ones left the Church of England at various times for conscience' sake; the Methodists separated from the Church of England in circumstances which allow the blame to be allocated in various quarters by denominational historians. They have all been harassed in the past by the Church of England, and having as a result set up homes of their own and established their own identities, they have no wish to be simply re-absorbed by their Mother Church, any more than the Church of England wishes to be simply re-absorbed by Rome.

Until the time of the First World War, few of these, whether Roman Catholics or Protestants, would have contemplated the disappearance or humiliation of the Church of England with anything but equanimity, even satisfaction. Times have changed since then, and such an attitude has vanished. But it is still true that every non-Anglican Christian in England must ask at least once in a lifetime, and ask searchingly, whether the Church of England as we know it is really entitled to the status, influence and prestige which it possesses. This book is the record of one Free Churchman's enquiry into this question, and the enquiry is bound to be wide-ranging, covering the Establishment and many other issues as well.

There are many things about the Church of England which Free Church people of our time admire, love and sometimes envy, and the examples of these that follow by no means exhaust the tally that could be drawn up.

We greatly respect its strong sense of continuity as a living embodiment of the Christian past. To enter a cathedral or a parish church is to be reminded at once of the longevity, breadth and richness of Christian history. It soon becomes apparent in most cases that the building itself, and the Christian worship that has taken place in it, and the Christian devotion that the worship has inspired, reach far back into the past, especially when it is notified that 'this church was first built in' the fourteenth, thirteenth, twelfth, or eleventh century, or even before the Conquest. Even when the essential simplicity of an Anglican structure is obscured by Victorian imitativeness, or overlaid with adornment, the atmosphere and the awareness of continuity remain. And for myself, when I was once present at an Ordination in Winchester Cathedral, at a particularly bleak period of Christian witness in the sixties, I was deeply imbued with the consciousness – which may or may not be true to the facts – that the ancient and majestic Church of England, rooted in the past, lives on serenely and securely in the present and into the uncertain future. A similar consciousness is not aroused by any non-Anglican building.

And here it is right that a Free Churchman should pay tribute to the Tractarians, whom Free Church people do not usually approve. For it is to them that all of us, Anglicans and others, owe the vivid awareness of church history as stretching back into the centuries of the Christian past before there was an English Church or an English nation. It is worth noticing how they achieved this.

English people, especially in a nationalistic era like our own, are prone to think that what happens in their country far surpasses in importance anything that happens elsewhere. Richard Hooker, William Laud (in his own way), the Caroline Divines and John Wesley had tried to reawaken a consciousness of catholic history, but not with entire success. The Tractarians, convinced that the Church of England is the Catholic Church in these islands and is in all important respects identical with the Primitive Church,[1] set about preserving the 'holy tradition' by collecting, translating, editing and expounding the writings of the Fathers, with the express purpose of recalling Anglicans to their true destiny.[2]

Of course, much of this historical writing was not very objective; it was indeed a *re*-writing, an unconscious tailoring of church history in the early days, and then of English church history, to suit Tractarian presuppositions. Cyprian of Carthage turned out to be a good and powerful Anglican bishop in a thin disguise. The fiery and obstinate Athanasius materialized from the shadows of the past as a model of gentle but persistent Victorian piety and orthodoxy. But this was natural in the circumstances, and in due course produced the necessary reaction in the form of a much more critical appraisal of the documents, starting with the work of B. H. Streeter, an Anglican of a different school of thought, who decided that the history of early Christianity which had been served up to him was not history at all,[3] and needed to be sharply scrutinized. Subsequent Anglican historians have taken due note of his warning, and the old romanticism has largely gone, while the good effects remain.

Thus by a kind of dialectical process the Church of England through its scholars of different and often conflicting schools of thought has provided as accurate an account of the early church as we are likely to have, and has put this particular part of the Christian heritage at the disposal of all English Christians.

All this history belongs, of course, equally to all Christians of every church, and English Christianity from the beginning is as much a part of the Roman Catholic, Nonconformist and Methodist heritage as it is of Anglicanism. But it is Anglicans who have brought it alive for the rest of us.

Book-learning is not by any means all that the Church of England has supplied for the preservation of the Christian heritage. Even more important is its orderly worship, which seems to reach back into the dim recesses of the past and is yet relevant to the present age. It has always been a matter of legitimate Anglican pride that whatever may be the theological fashions or social customs of the age, whatever may be the liturgical idiosyncracies, or even the partial heresies or personal peculiarities, of the incumbent, the worship of the parish church goes on, constant and unhurried; and both the regular worshippers from the locality and visiting strangers can be immediately at home with the noble words, the sober vestments and the solemn action, sanctioned by long usage, which they will encounter wherever they enter church on Sunday or at the appointed times for weekday prayer or sacrament. There are, of course, exceptions even to this, but not the alarming variation found in the Free Churches, from the monotony of often-repeated but officially extemporaneous prayers, often of inordinate length, to the studied improvizations which seem to be designed to fix the congregation's attention on the person in the pulpit. Non-Anglican worship can attain heights of personal and sometimes corporate devotion, and of homiletical excellence, rarely found in Anglicanism; it can also sink to depths of dreariness or sentimentality, or mere verbosity, which no Anglican congregation would tolerate.

It has to be remembered that the Wesleys, when they gathered people together to hear the exposition of scripture and sing the hymns which were based on scriptural doctrines, presupposed attendance at the regular services, and especially the eucharists, of the parish church. Methodist worship began, not as an independent expression of Christian devotion, but as a complement to established Anglican liturgy – with the admixture, no doubt, of protest against the formalism which was unfortunately prevalent at the time. After the separation of Anglicans and Methodists, the Methodists were left without the liturgical infra-structure of Anglicanism, though by retaining the Book of Common Prayer's Order of Holy Communion, only slightly modified, and, in many places for many years, Anglican Matins, many of them did their best to hold on to it. This is why in these days many Methodists wish to regain what they have lost, without ceasing to be Methodists.[4] So they greatly value the Anglican liturgy.

It may seem singular to emphasize the continuity of liturgical tradition in the Church of England just at the time when that church has suffered a liturgical sea-change. After all, it may be said, the Book of Common Prayer has been abandoned and the Alternative Service Book has taken its place. In particular, it is alleged the superb language of the one has been supplanted by the banal vernacular of the other.

But the facts are not quite as stated. The Book of Common Prayer was written in the common language of the sixteenth and seventeenth centuries as it was spoken by the educated classes. By a kind of miracle it was touched with a splendour and a resonance that the English language, in all its changes, has not subsequently achieved. It thus succeeded in expressing the religious thoughts and aspirations of English people for a much longer period of years than scholars of language would normally have thought possible. But by the third decade of this century it was beginning to be meaningless to those who lacked the historical background which could have enabled them to interpret and apply it.

Then came the discovery, by Anglican and other scholars, that the eucharistic liturgy in the Prayer Book, for all its great merits, was deficient in one doctrine (that of the resurrection), over-emphatic on another (that of the atonement), and irreconcileable with the eucharistic pattern which could be traced back to the earliest celebrations. The last point was amply documented and persuasively argued by Gregory Dix in *The Shape of the Liturgy*, 1945, another masterpiece of Anglican historical scholarship. Once the thesis of this book had made its way into the consciousness of Anglican thinkers and leaders, it was only a matter of time before the Order of Holy Communion came to be revised – and, for good measure, many of the other services as well.

The revisers set about their difficult task with the determination to restore the fourfold shape of the eucharist which goes back in essence to the actions of Jesus at the Last Supper: 'he took bread, he gave thanks, and broke it; and he gave it to them' (Luke 22.19). They also restored the doctrinal balance, and increased the participation of the faithful; and for the verbal parts they used the common language of the late twentieth century as it is spoken by the educated people of today (much more numerous than in the sixteenth and seventeenth centuries). By acting in this way they revived many ancient traditions while discarding some modern ones, mainly in the area of language. It could be that twentieth-century English is not a suitable vehicle for Christian liturgy – this will not be known until several generations have passed away – but it was the one that had to be used in order that modern Christians could share in the traditions of the past; and in practice, against the odds and in spite of occasional infelicities, the Church of England, partly by the ample use of scriptural phrases and ideas, has thus preserved its continuity with the past, except for those who prefer beautiful sound to Christian meaning. To attend an Anglican eucharist is still, as ever, to be taken up into the communion of the saints in heaven as well as those on earth.[5]

One particular element in Anglican worship should not go

without special mention, however. The role of hymns is rather ambiguous. Often they seem to have no direct relation to the point in the liturgy which has been reached, and to invite only the half-hearted attention of the congregation. Yet it is in the hymns of George Herbert, Thomas Ken and John Keble that the sober but searching spirit of traditional Anglican piety is most tellingly expressed. A Methodist might say: 'If only Ken's

> Let all thy converse be sincere,
> Thy conscience as the noonday clear;
> Think how all-seeing God thy ways
> And all thy secret thoughts surveys.
>
> Lord, I my vows to thee renew;
> Scatter my sins as morning dew;
> Guard my first springs of thought and will,
> And with thyself my spirit fill

could be complemented by Charles Wesley's

> My heart is full of Christ, and longs
>   Its glorious matter to declare!
> Of him I make my loftier songs,
>   I cannot from his praise forbear;
> My ready tongue makes haste to sing
> The glories of my heavenly King,

then we should have congregational singing which married mind and heart.' This hymn of Wesley's is not in any Anglican hymn book. But we are learning more and more to sing each other's hymns, and its time will come.

The Church of England has very great intellectual and spiritual resources. This is to be expected of what is by far the largest church in the country, but there is more to it than mere numbers. Until just over a century ago, the Church of England had a virtual monopoly of access to the universities of Oxford, Cambridge and Durham, and to the theological schools of these universities until much more recently; Free Church people had to be content with the facilities offered, in the eighteenth century by the far from negligible but small, Religious Academies, and in the nineteenth century and later by such seminaries and schools as they could themselves maintain – except that some Free Churchmen were willing to conform to the Church of England for the sake of their education. This has given Anglican teachers a very long start in theological scholarship of every kind, and it is not possible for the Free Churches, even if they wish to do so, to catch up.

But there is a deeper reason even than that. The Anglican emphasis on reason, not as the opponent but as the partner of faith, has created an openness to new ideas, and, in modern times, an acceptance of critical methods when applied to the Bible, the creeds and church history, which has been an example to other denominations which sometimes, it must be admitted, they have been reluctant to follow. There have been periods of resistance to intellectual change, as when the theory of evolution seemed to strike at the vitals of the faith, and periods of cold rationalism, as when Anglicans could not stomach the emotionalism (pejoratively called 'enthusiasm') of the early Methodists. But by and large Anglican reasonableness, not untinged with controlled emotion, has produced a sequence of constructive thinkers which runs from Richard Hooker and the Caroline Divines through Joseph Butler and George Berkeley to John Henry Newman, F. D. Maurice, Charles Gore, William Temple and Michael Ramsey – not to speak of a host of others from whom it would be invidious to select. It is in Anglicanism (except perhaps for Newman, in part) that their work was done and in Anglicanism that it has been most fully appreciated and appropriated. In the ecumenical age this treasure house also has been progressively opened to the rest of us; and, in particular, for a whole long generation, William Temple was 'the Doctor of the Church' for us all without discrimination.

The keeping of the festivals, great and small, is characteristic of Anglican continuity with the past, and the list of 'Lesser Festivals and Commemorations', included in the calendar at the beginning of the Alternative Service Book is highly instructive. It comprises more than eighty entries, mostly relating to individuals, but some to groups (where names are not given) or pairs of people (where they are). Among them are mentioned twelve people who would be generally regarded as 'Anglican saints', only one of whom is a woman (Josephine Butler); John and Charles Wesley are also there, but the Church of England makes no exclusive claim to them; and so is Charles I, to whom sainthood may be denied by many, and martyrdom by some.

The twelve Anglicans (in order of annual celebration) are George Herbert, Edward King, Thomas Ken, William Law, William Wilberforce, Jeremy Taylor, Lancelot Andrews, James Hannington, Richard Hooker, Charles Simeon, Nicholas Ferrar and Josephine Butler. These are no doubt representative of the various types of Anglican spirituality – Charles Simeon of pastoral and prophetic evangelicalism, William Wilberforce and Josephine Butler of social reform, James Hannington of missionary zeal, Richard Hooker of apologetic brilliance. The others – Herbert, King, Ken, Law, Taylor, Andrews, and Ferrar – represent the sober, scholarly, sacramental, corporate piety which marks out the Church of England at its best. This piety also acts as an inspiration and a corrective to those in other denominations who miss the solid, apparently imperishable framework of architecture, liturgy and order which the Church of England possesses. It is not an accident that one of the most moving literary tributes to Edward King is by the Methodist John Newton, who quotes at the end of his book the collect for King's day, 8 March, as conveying 'the quintessence of this quiet English saint':[6]

O Almighty God, who gavest such grace unto thy servant Edward King that whomsoever he met, he drew nearer to thee: Fill us, we beseech thee, with sympathy as tender and as deep, that we also may win others to know the love which passeth knowledge; through Jesus Christ thy Son our Lord. Amen.

Anglicans on the whole renounce, or mildly disclaim, any excessive intensity of devotion or religious experience. They are able to do so because the spiritual life of their church is sustained, perhaps without the knowledge of the generality of church members, by the absolute commitment to Christian ideals and practice, as Anglicans understand them, of the religious communities, both

of men and of women; these owe much to their Roman counterparts, no doubt, but have a distinctively Anglican flavour. And it
is not least the members of these communities who are able to
conduct the retreats which nourish the personal devotion of many
'ordinary' Anglican people and many Anglican priests.

For most Anglicans, much of what has been said so far, though
they will perhaps grant its importance, is (as they would say) 'far
above their heads'. Their concern is the local parish church and its
activities. The parish system goes back immemorially into English
history; and still today the parish priest believes himself to be
entrusted with 'the cure of souls' in the particular geographical
area which is his parish. He may quickly conclude that he cannot
fully carry out his allotted task; he may be willing to share it with
his non-Anglican colleagues; but he cannot rid himself of his inner
responsibility. Good or bad? Bad, when he makes the parish his
world, sinks into parochialism and leads his flock into the same
quagmire. Good, when he includes in his prayers and love all
those who live on his patch, with all their varying concerns.
While that good remains, the parish church is still the place to
which the people naturally come on corporate occasions, and
where they feel at home, even those who usually worship elsewhere or nowhere; it is still a place of refreshment for every
parishioner and visitor, Anglican or not.

There is another element in Anglican life, very different from
the others in character, for which non-Anglicans ought to be
grateful to the Church of England, though not all of them are. It
is the continuing contribution of that church to general English
culture. Cathedral music is an obvious and excellent example of
this; it is a vital part of English musical life, and draws into its
orbit as performers, singers and auditors many Free Church people
and many people who belong to no Church at all. The same is
true, though to a much reduced extent, of drama performed in
parish churches and cathedrals. In the plastic and pictorial arts the
Anglican achievement is plain for all to see.

Nowadays it is hard to discern many traces of Anglican influence
in university life, except in the theological faculties, which
Anglicans share with Free Church scholars, and in the College

chapels of Oxbridge and some university chapels elsewhere; but in the past the Church of England did more to shape university education in this country than any other single institution. Some will regret this now, and some will rejoice, but the fact remains. Anglican public schools, like other independent schools, are now under fire; but the best of them have provided, and still provide, models of education and community which modern educationalists would be foolish to disregard. 'Church schools' for the young have been sources of educational and ecclesiastical division in the past, and may be so still in some areas. But they were pioneers in the field, and by constant adaptation to modern needs and possibilities they have retained their high standards.

It is often said that the principal glory of the Church of England is its comprehensiveness. Of course, it is not comprehensive in the sense in which Elizabeth I wished it to be. Her own efforts in that direction failed, and the subsequent civil and religious strife, culminating in the Clarendon Code, postponed that kind of comprehensiveness into the indefinite future. Only in our time has the effort been renewed in a different form, and we still have not discovered the way to reach the goal.

Nevertheless the comprehensiveness of the Church of England is real, in the sense that it comprehends all English Christians who accept episcopacy and do not accept the authority of the Roman See in this country. This means that a clergyman of strong evangelical principles who detests all 'Romish' practices and regards his parish as an outpost of Geneva, but gives canonical obedience to his bishop, is truly an Anglican. So is one who regards the Catholic Church as consisting solely of the Roman Catholic Church, the Orthodox Churches and the Church of England, accepts all the doctrines of the Roman Catholic Church, except that of the world-wide jurisdiction and infallibility of the Pope, but acknowledges the bishops of the Church of England as being in the apostolic succession. The great majority of Anglican priests, who embrace neither of these extremes, but stand somewhere between them, differing widely in theology and liturgical practice, are easily included. So with the laity: the congregations of both extremist views, as well as those who profess no allegiance to either, and indeed in many cases wish for nothing more than moderation in all things, are all generously comprehended within the ambit of the Ecclesia Anglicana.

This has the effect that, apart from episcopacy, the varieties of Free Church faith and life, especially in the case of the Methodists, fall doctrinally and liturgically between the Anglican extremes, so that if the problem of episcopacy could be solved, the Church of England could contain them all, if this were desired by all parties; it means also that many Free Church people, again especially the Methodists, have more in common with the central block of Anglicans than the two wings of Anglicanism have with each other.

But its most evident effect is that within the Church of England itself Anglicans of very different persuasions use the same rites and ceremonies – this is just as true in relation to the Alternative Service Book as with the Book of Common Prayer – and, in particular, the same words and actions at the very heart of the eucharistic liturgy. They would offer markedly different theological interpretations, but they use the same liturgy. The next most evident effect is that episcopacy, although very differently expounded in different quarters by theologians, clergy and laypeople, and indeed by the bishops themselves, is accepted and valued by all. This illustrates the built-in inclusiveness of Anglican worship and practice, and it makes all the more puzzling the fact that when a similar inclusiveness was made part of the Service of Reconciliation in the Anglican-Methodist Scheme, it was rejected so angrily by Evangelicals and Anglo-Catholics. The Anglican inclusiveness is intended to reconcile and hold together those who agree on main principles but differ on doctrinal implications.[7]

This comprehensiveness is in many respects admirable and enviable. Its theological difficulties for the present time will be discussed later, but let it be said now that a balance of doctrine, though sometimes precarious, has certainly been preserved from the Reformation until now, partly by the Thirty-Nine Articles. The unity of the Church of Christ to be prayed and worked for is a unity in diversity, as is being more and more clearly seen by ecumenists,[8] and it is of great value both to the Church of England

and to the churches that seek closer relations with it that this principle is positively and successfully embodied, here and now, in this country. Plainly the diversity must have some limits if it is not to devalue the unity and dissolve into vagueness, and this matter must always be one of concern to Anglicans and others. But to set the principle on one side because of its dangers would be to divide Christendom into exclusive sects and make even ultimate unity impossible.

The comprehensiveness of the Church of England ensures, moreover, that disagreements on doctrine and ethics and worship are explored and discussed, and if possible resolved, within the confines of one church, and not across denominational boundaries. They should therefore be easier to deal with constructively, and if this does not always turn out to be the case in every church the fault must surely lie, not with the conditions of the discussion but with the sectarianism of some or all of the participants, leading them to insist on the last letter of their particular dogma.

This has always been the contention of ecumenists when they have been met with the assertion that doctrinal unity on all matters must be reached and guaranteed before churches can unite. They have said: 'let us by all means, and of course, agree on essentials; other matters are best dealt with when we are united. If we discuss them before we are united, or at least covenanted together, agreement, or agreement to differ, will be hampered by the intrusion of extraneous elements, in the shape of denominational pride and denominational conventions.' The Church of England has the potentiality of being a living demonstration of this contention and an example to all the world.

The question has to be asked: what is it that keeps the Church of England together in spite of its diversity, and its sometimes quite obviously painful internal conflicts? The answer that was current a generation ago was that it was the Book of Common Prayer which achieved this remarkable feat; and no doubt the fear that liturgical reform may rend the church apart is one of the things that motivate the doughty opponents of the Alternative Service Book. But the relative disuse of the Book of Common Prayer cannot really be said to be disrupting the church, though it has led to some acute controversies. The Book of Common Prayer can still be used, after all, where it is desired. It is 'common prayer' as such, i.e. worshipping in much the same form everywhere, which helps to cement the Church of England, not the Book of Common Prayer itself.

Others would claim that the really uniting force is the Establishment, which we shall discuss fully as this book proceeds. It may be, again, that fear of the divisive consequences of disestablishment has prevented many important reforms in the area of church and state. It may even be that in moments of great internal crisis the Anglican desire not to be disowned by the state has kept intact links between Anglicans which would otherwise have been severed. But the fact that disestablishment is now once again being actively considered by those who set high store on their church's unity seems to indicate the possibility that a disestablished church might have a still deeper and better unity than exists at present, even though the numerical size of that Church might be diminished.

It remains to be concluded that the most effective, though not the only cohesive force is episcopacy. Not, let us hasten to add, a particular doctrine of episcopacy, for, as we have seen, many various doctrines are held by Anglicans; and not, certainly, a rigid doctrine of apostolic succession, for this has been held only at certain periods of Anglican history, and then only by some, and is not held widely today – unless of course it is maintained that the succession in this sense acts *ex opere operato*, even when no one believes in it. No, it is the *fact* of episcopacy that binds the church together. All churches have some form of *episcope* – the care and oversight of the church – even those who limit its operation to the local congregation. For Methodists *episcope* resides in the Conference, which is a kind of corporate bishop, and is exercised on behalf of the Conference by District Chairmen and Circuit Superintendents. The United Reformed Church holds to an even more conciliar form of episcope. In the Church of England, and the other churches of the Anglican Communion, and, by agreement between the uniting churches, in the Churches of South India and North India, it is exercised by a person. This is a more significant fact in Anglican churches and the united churches than it is in the Roman Catholic Church, which has a much more centralized administration than an Anglican church ever has.

The system of personal bishops can be, and has been sometimes, corrupted into prelacy; it can be blunted and hampered, as it frequently now is in the Church of England, by an overweight of administrative chores. It can even be virtually disregarded by clergy who treat their parishes as private empires where the writ of the bishop no doubt runs, but can be skilfully evaded. The leadership of the bishops, even when acting together, can be rejected by those who in the next breath salute the bishops as the guardians of the faith and practice of the Church of England. But the fact of the bishop in his diocese remains the strong link between all the Anglicans who live within his area. He brings to them and interprets the apostolic tradition which they inherit, and the particular tradition of the Church of England. He is pastor to clergy and people; he is the point of reference on every major topic; he speaks in his Synod as the spokesman of the Church of England and of those churches with which it is in communion; he permits, forbids, dispenses and authorizes, in the cases submitted to him by clergy and parishes and individuals; he confirms, ordains and appoints, and when he presides at the eucharist the occasion has a special, indeed unique solemnity. If he is lax or tyrannical or remote or partisan, this can be tolerated until his successor comes; for the office, not the man in whom it is temporarily incarnate, is what ultimately counts, however much the acceptability of the man affects the quality of the respect and obedience which are granted to him. Commissions and Working Parties have sat, sit and will continue to sit, on the role of the bishop, the size of dioceses and many other related matters. Meanwhile the bishop holds together the people, the groups which would otherwise go their separate ways, and the institutions which might otherwise fall apart, including the Church of England itself. And of this the Free Churches are taking, and should be taking, increasingly respectful notice, now that they can look at bishops with eyes undimmed by the harassments and misunderstandings of the past.

These are some of the strengths of the Church of England. Can we say that with its notable history and sense of history, its deep inner life, its wide influence, and its immense resources, both tangible and intangible, this church is making its greatest possible contribution to the whole Church of God and the life of this nation? Or do its weaknesses make it impossible for this to happen?

2

Constitutional Anomalies

The history of England, and most of all the replacement of the Pope's jurisdiction by that of the Tudor monarchs, has helped to give to the Church of England a unique constitution. The framework of that constitution and its details are fascinating to the historian, and endow the church with some of the rich traditionalism of which it is justly proud. But they contain some anomalies which cannot be justified by purely historical considerations.

We take first the matter of worship. Very few of those attending divine service in the Church of England on any Sunday are aware that the words and actions used for prayer and the celebration of the sacraments are under the ultimate control of Parliament, as once they were under the control of the Crown. It is just as well that the majority of churchgoers remain in ignorance of this fact, since an impediment to sincere and wholehearted worship is thus removed; while those who are aware of the situation have presumably come to terms with it in their own minds, and so are not hindered by it from worshipping truly.

Yet, coldly considered, it is an extraordinary state of affairs. Not so extraordinary as the situation before the Enabling Act of 1919; until then not the slightest alteration to any part of the Book of Common Prayer could be made without the explicit approval of Parliament after debate. Since 1919 any proposals for the alteration of liturgy may be deposited on the table of Parliament, and, if no member of Parliament asks for a debate within thirty days the authorized bodies (authorized, that is, by Parliament) of the Church of England are at liberty to put the proposals into effect. The Worship and Doctrine Measure of 1975 has extended this liberty. The good sense of Parliament has on the whole prevailed in the matter, and allowed the church to make the liturgical changes which it thinks proper; but not in the notorious case of the revisions to the Book of Common Prayer which had been approved by all the constitutional bodies of the church, and were then rejected by the House of Commons, in 1927, and again, despite some mild changes, in 1928. It seems unlikely that such a disaster will be repeated, but it remains the case that the House of Commons (of whose members only a minority are devout Anglicans, or even Anglicans of any sort, and the majority, apart from Free Church people, are probably agnostic or atheist), has not renounced its final authority over the forms of worship to be used in the Church of England, and in certain circumstances might exercise that authority.

The Canon Law exhibits many peculiarities. But it must first be described. *The Canons of the Church of England*, known for short as Canon Law, are binding on the clergy and those lay people who hold office within the Church. They are not, strictly, part of the law of England, except for certain of them which were enacted before the Reformation and were retained after it as not being repugnant to the new form of the church or to the prerogatives of the Crown. The rest, which have reached their present formulation and content as a result of extensive revision in 1964 and 1969, and smaller changes since then, are, according to Halsbury's *Ecclesiastical Law*, 'in part directives for the guidance of the church and in part subsidiary legislation'. The revisions of 1964 and 1969 were approved and enacted by the Houses of Convocation; subsequent revisions by the General Synod set up in 1970. The Synod acts on such revisions in three stages: General Approval, Revision, and Final Approval, and normally one stage only is taken in any series of sessions. For Final Approval a two-thirds majority is usually required in all three houses of the Synod – the House of Bishops, the House of Clergy and the House of Laity.

The Canons are not laid before Parliament, but the Queen's assent and licence are required before a new Canon is promulged, i.e. brought into operation. Therefore after the Synod has given its Final Approval to any new or revised Canon, the text is sent to the Home Office in order to ensure that it does not contravene the 'customs, laws and statutes of the realm' or 'the prereogatives of the Crown', and then goes to the Queen for her signature.

The Canons are enforceable on clergy and office-holding lay-people, not in the courts of the land, but in the courts of the church. Such enforcement takes place very rarely. It is left to the bishops to make such enforcement unnecessary by their pastoral counsel, exhortation and (no doubt, occasionally) warning.

All this may be very distant from the New Testament, and indeed there are no texts which can be adduced in direct support. There is nothing unique or discreditable about this fact. No sensible Christians expect the Church of England, or any other church, to be governed and regulated in the uncomplicated ways which were appropriate to the early churches in Jerusalem, Rome and on the shores of the Mediterranean. These ways indeed are by no means followed even by those churches who claimed, after the Reformation, to return to biblical simplicity. Some of them indeed may have constitutions which are simpler in outline, but this is because they have not been so closely involved as the Church of England in the political and social history of the English nation. The Methodist Church today indeed, in spite of this, has 987 Standing Orders (with functions, of course, rather different from that of Canon Law).

But a peculiarity is to be observed when Canon C1, 'Of Holy Orders in the Church of England', asserts, in order to uphold the ordering of the church, 'that from the Apostles' time there have been these orders in Christ's church: bishops, priests and deacons', and 'that the Church of England holds and teaches' this particular version of early church history (the assertion occurs also in the Preface to the 1662 Ordinal, but not in the Ordinal of the Alternative Service Book). Scarcely any responsible historian, Anglican or other, nowadays accepts this version. It is odd that it should still appear in the Canon Law.

The majority of the Canons are, properly, profitably and understandably, concerned with the ordained ministry in its multifarious aspects – selection, training, ordination, institution, induction, appointment, hierarchy, authority, down to detailed instructions about the vestures to be worn in the conduct of divine worship. All these matters – not least that of 'vestures' – have aroused disputes in the church from time to time, and it can reasonably be hoped that the careful formulation and re-formulation of Canons in the last twenty years will put an end to such disputes; and in any case further revisions are possible.

The remaining Canons give a first impression of a random selection of subjects for legislation. But no doubt in each apparently eccentric case the reason for inclusion is a controversy or other crisis in the past. Presumably the requirement of Canon B132 that 'in every cathedral church the dean or provost, the canons residentiary, and the other ministers of the church, being in Holy Orders, shall all receive the Holy Communion every Sunday at the least, except they have a reasonable cause to the contrary', springs from the failure in the past of certain cathedral dignitaries to avail themselves of their eucharistic opportunities. Yet is it really necessary to retain this requirement in legislative form at the present day? This Canon could surely have gone the way of the 'Declaration against Simony', which since the reforms of the 1960s it has not been necessary for deans and other such persons to recite at their installation. But it remains on the statute book.

Another slightly odd Canon is B9 'Of Reverence and Attention to be used in the time of Divine Service', in which it is laid down that 'All persons present in the time of divine service shall in the due place audibly with the minister say the General Confession, the Lord's Prayer and the Creed, and make the answers appointed in the form of service.' 'Divine Service' includes, as is clear from the preceding Canon, Morning and Evening Prayer and the Holy Communion. Yet at a Choral Eucharist it is often impossible for the congregation to say or even sing the creed *audibly*, as when the choir sings this part of the service in a setting which discourages congregational participation.

These last are no doubt fairly trivial matters, easily put right. There are more serious matters about which questions need to be asked, and three of them can be here specified. They all relate to the present ecumenical situation, the first two directly, the third indirectly.

Canon B15A states:

1. There shall be admitted to the Holy Communion:

(a) members of the Church of England who have been confirmed in accordance with the rites of that Church or are ready and desirous to be so confirmed or who have been otherwise episcopally confirmed with unction or the laying on of hands, except as provided by the next following Canon;

(b) baptized persons who are communicant members of other churches which subscribe to the doctrine of the Holy Trinity, and who are in good standing in their own church;

(c) any other baptized persons authorized to be admitted under regulations of the General Synod; and

(d) any baptized person in immediate danger of death.

2. If any person by virtue of sub paragraph (b) above regularly receives the Holy Communion over a long period which appears likely to continue indefinitely, the minister shall set before him the normal requirements of the Church of England for communicant status in that church.

We leave on one side the difficulty, often pointed out, of defining the term 'members of the Church of England', especially as it refers to unconfirmed persons. Canon B15A was approved by the General Synod in 1974 in the aftermath of the double rejection by the Church of England of the Anglican-Methodist Scheme for union in two stages, and went some way, in clause 1 (b), towards healing the grievous hurt inflicted on members of the Methodist Church by that rejection. It was, and is, welcomed by Free Church people, as an effective sign of ecumenical intentions.

But in the years since its enactment certain limitations have become evident. It bestows on Free Church people the status of guests, and indeed of honoured and welcome guests, at Anglican eucharists. It is particularly acceptable to those Free Church people who in the past wished to share from time to time in the sacramental life of the Church of England, as they hoped that Anglicans would share in theirs, but were perplexed as to whether to present themselves at an Anglican eucharist. But there are many other Free Church people who find themselves permanently living in a community where there is no church of their own denomination, or where the eucharist according to the rites of their church is celebrated only rarely, because of a shortage in ministerial man and womanpower, and are therefore eager to receive communion in the parish church regularly and 'for a long period which appears likely to continue indefinitely'. They are admitted to Holy Communion as guests, but only as guests; they can never count themselves as 'members of the family', which is what they wish and in their hearts believe themselves to be. Is the Church of England really content with this situation?

In due course the parish priest may, and no doubt should, in accordance with clause 2 of the Canon, set before such people 'the normal requirements of the Church of England for communicant status'. This must mean that he is to suggest that they should be episcopally confirmed. In some cases, of course, they may be happy to be so confirmed; in others, they may agree to be so confirmed for the sake of their own sacramental life; in others they will be bound to refuse because of their profound conviction that they are already communicant members of the Holy Catholic Church and cannot, in conscience, go back on that. In the last case it is difficult to see what should subsequently happen if the Canon is to be observed.

In all three cases the Church of England is asking members of the church of Christ to imply by their actions that they have not so far been members of that church in the fullest sense. And this will not do. Theologically, they are members of the church of Christ by baptism; they have confirmed and (as the Presbyterians say) 'improved' their membership, and prayed for the confirming power of the Spirit, in the rite of confirmation used in their own church, unless they have become members by 'believers' baptism', and sometimes by confirmation in that case also. It is not laid down anywhere in the New Testament that confirmation, to be 'valid', needs to be episcopal, nor is this held to be so throughout the universal church, but only in some parts of it: the Roman Catholic Church, for instance, allows presbyteral confirmation in certain situations, and has recently increased the number of such situations. Moreover, so far as the Church of England is concerned, although the admission of Methodists not episcopally confirmed to Holy Communion was a matter of dispute when the Anglican-Methodist Scheme was under consideration, it was not raised as an objection to the recent Covenanting Proposals which provided for it.

It is sometimes urged that the requirement of episcopal confirmation is a matter of Anglican discipline rather than doctrine. But this discipline was formulated and imposed in a very different historical situation from the present, at a time when nonconformists expressed their nonconformity by refusing to present themselves for episcopal confirmation. There is no question now of 'expressing nonconformity', but only the wish to be drawn into closer unity by mutual recognition of membership. If it is only 'discipline' which stands in the way of that, then surely doctrine should prevail over discipline. And the necessary doctrinal basis is provided by the nature and intention of the rite of confirmation (sometimes under other names) as practised in the Free Churches. Most people who scrutinize these will cease to doubt this statement.

But some would say, on theological grounds, that the defect in Free Church confirmation is that the minister who carries it out is himself not episcopally ordained. This indeed represents a tenable theological viewpoint, which lies at the root of the recent failures to make advance towards unity. But it cannot properly be adduced at this point, since Canon B15A already allows for those confirmed by non-episcopally ordained ministers to receive communion at Anglican altars for a prolonged period – indeed for an indefinite period in the cases where clause 2 of the Canon is not applied; and indeed usually even when it is applied, for the Canon does not require the priest to exclude from communion those who are not willing to be confirmed and probably very few priests practise such exclusion. Thus the doctrinal pass has already been sold – as some would put it.

The practical solution to this problem is usually found by simply neglecting clause 2 of Canon B15A. In fact it is not easy to find examples of its being brought into effect. This is a scarcely satisfactory situation. Should not the clause be repealed as soon as possible?

There is another, even stronger, reason for its repeal. There are more than four hundred 'Local Ecumenical Projects' in England – a development in the mission and towards the unity of the church in this country which is highly significant for the Church of England as well as for the other churches involved, but which is not mentioned in any of the Canons. In these Projects the churches taking part – most often the Parish Church and the Methodist Church, but in many cases also the United Reformed Church, the Baptist Church and the Moravian Church, and in some cases the Roman Catholic Church – covenant together in a very solemn manner 'to build up a common life of worship and fellowship', and to 'share in mission through the confession of one faith in teaching, witness and service to the community' (according to the formula proposed in the *Bristol Handbook to Local Ecumenical Projects*, and widely adopted). Sometimes the worship of all the Christians sharing in the project takes place in one building at all times (the building being held in common under a Sharing Agreement); sometimes two or more buildings are used, sometimes for denominational worship, sometimes for united worship. In all cases, so far as is known, the members of all the participating churches freely share in the eucharist, whether the president be a Free Church minister or an Anglican priest, whether the building be Anglican or Free Church. Such eucharistic sharing is plainly essential to the whole life of the Project, and is experienced by all as the wholly appropriate embodiment of the unity which the Project acknowledges and promotes. The eucharistic rite that is used is nearly always that of the church in which the service takes place. There is no doubt that the laypeople in the Project come to regard all the ordained ministers in the 'ecumenical team' as *their* pastors, ministers and priests, without distinction of denomination.

Since about 1975 the practice of 'joint confirmation', according to a form composed in Bristol and approved by the House of Bishops and the proper authorities in the other churches, has spread rapidly. Candidates for confirmation receive the laying-on-of-hands *both* from the Anglican bishop *and* from a minister of each of the other churches participating in the Project, and thereby become communicant members, with full rights, of all the churches taking part. They are thus able, so long as they remain in the area of the Project, to receive Holy Communion without any restriction, in any of the churches of the Project (if they move into another area, they are normally required to opt for one or other of the denominations of which they have become members).

Those in Local Ecumenical Projects who had been confirmed in non-Anglican churches before their Project was set up could receive communion at Anglican altars even before the time of Canon B15A, since by a bishops' ruling 'Areas of Ecumenical Experiment' (as LEPs were then called) could be regarded as 'standing conferences for Christian unity', at which such reception of communion was permitted. Now they are able to receive communion under Canon B15A. But it is as *guests* that they are admitted – guests in their own home, since the Project is the spiritual home of all its members. No one, presumably, would venture to bring clause 2 of the Canon into operation in their case!

Pending the urgently necessary repeal of clause 2 – this could not be carried out in a moment because of the nature of Anglican procedures and the probability of opposition – a plan for 'Extended Membership' has been put forward, and could presumably be carried out, after the agreement of the House of Bishops, by those who are willing. This entails the issuing of an official certificate to all the senior churchmembers in the Local Ecumenical Project, whatever their denomination, to the effect that they have the full rights of membership in all the denominations sharing in the Project so long as they live within its boundaries. This could certainly ease the pastoral situation, and at the same time go a little way towards the mutual recognition of which the Local Ecumenical Projects wish to be the pioneers.

But the repeal of clause 2 is not sufficient for all the purposes of a Local Ecumenical Project. The status of 'guest communicant' is just not proper for those who wish to take a full part in the life of the Project. The whole of the Canon needs to be looked at, and to be revised, shortened, or added to, in such a way as to acknowledge and approve the reality by which the members of all the Churches involved already receive the Holy Communion together without reservations or questions in their minds.

Canon C15 prescribes that every archbishop and bishop on the occasions both of his consecration and of his enthronement, and every person to be ordained priest or deacon on the occasions both of his ordination and of each subsequent 'institution, admission to a benefice or licensing to a curacy', shall make and subscribe 'the Declaration of Assent'. The making and subscription of this Declaration follows the recital of a Preface which claims for the Church of England that it is part of the One, Holy Catholic and Apostolic Church, professes the faith uniquely revealed in the holy scriptures and bears witness to it in its historic formularies. At the end of the recital the archbishop, bishop, priest or deacon is asked whether he will affirm his 'loyalty to this inheritance of faith', and accept it as his 'inspiration and guidance under God in bringing the grace and truth of Christ to this generation and making him known to those in his care'.

To this question he responds: 'I, A.B., do so affirm, and accordingly declare my belief in the faith which is revealed in the holy scriptures and set forth in the catholic creeds and to which the historic formularies of the Church of England bear witness; and in public prayer and administration of the sacraments, I will use only the forms of service which are authorized or allowed by Canon.'

The Preface states the historic position of the Church of England, and does so without making any claims to the sole possession of Christian truth. The first half of the Declaration is rightly and properly expected of those who are to hold spiritual office in that church. And then suddenly, in the second half of the Declaration, we are confronted by an outbreak of restrictiveness and exclusiveness; for the only forms of service 'authorized by Canon' are those contained in the Book of Common Prayer and the Alternative Service Book (together with the service authorized by Royal Warrant for the anniversary of the Sovereign's accession), and the only services 'allowed by Canon', in addition to those which are authorized, are those approved by the Convocations of Canterbury and York for occasions for which no provision is made in either of those two books.

The purposes of this sentence in the Declaration are no doubt the preservation of the unity and distinctiveness of the Church of England in spite of all its diversity, and the elimination of liturgical practices which exceed the bounds of its comprehensiveness. It also helps to ensure that doctrine, which is implicit in any worship, is consonant with Anglican belief. But is it not now necessary to seek the accomplishment of these purposes by other means? For, as matters stand, it is a breach of the Declaration for any bishop, priest or deacon to lead (or, perhaps, even to take part in) any non-Anglican order of service, sacramental or other, not only in any Anglican place of worship, but in any place of worship or any other building, or in the open air.

This rules out episcopal participation in joint confirmation services and thus makes them either illegal or impossible. It insists that Anglican clergymen, invited as an ecumenical gesture, or as a way of friendly helping out in time of emergency, to conduct a service in a Free Church, must use an Anglican order of service. It descends with especially damaging force on Local Ecumenical Projects, where the imposition (not too strong a word) of an Anglican eucharistic liturgy on, shall we say, a United Reformed congregation would be taken not only as a sign of discourtesy but as an obstacle in the way of ecumenical progress; it would be taken equally amiss by a Methodist congregation which knew that the Methodist 'Sunday Service' is closely similar at all important points to the 'Order for Holy Communion Rite A'. It can safely be said that no Free Church minister invited in a Local Ecumenical Project to preside at the eucharist in an Anglican church would dream of using the Order of Service of his own denomination unless he were specifically asked to do so.

In practice, of course, the Declaration of Assent is breached at this point in many places every Sunday, and on other days of the week. Anglican priests preside at non-Anglican baptisms and eucharists; joint confirmation services are not only held but are increasing in number. Yet the Declaration of Assent is made solemnly, and in many cases fairly frequently, by every bishop and clergyman. Those who conscientiously carry out its prescriptions are painfully aware that they are putting a strain on good church and personal relations; those who disobey it on one set of conscientious grounds are painfully aware that they incur guilt on another set of conscientious grounds. And the bishops who are inclined to say that they would rather not be asked by their clergy whether or not to act in breach of the Declaration are not, probably, very comfortable either; and if they are asked have no option but to insist on adherence to the Declaration.[1]

All this undoubtedly amounts to saying that Local Ecumenical Projects, officially approved in principle by the Church of England, as by the other churches, and monitored in every case by a sponsoring body whose members have been appointed by their denominations for that purpose, are not receiving the support from the Church of England to which they are entitled. Should this not immediately be put right? It is good to know that the House of Bishops and the Board for Mission and Unity of the General Synod have set up a committee to make recommendations on this matter.[2]

But an even more important issue is at stake. Canon A8, 'Of Schisms', after stressing the evils of disunity and the grievous hindrances to the gospel which it creates, goes on thus: 'It is the duty of clergy and people to do their utmost not only to avoid occasions of strife but also to seek in penitence and brotherly charity to heal such divisions.' That double duty falls on the clergy and people of all denominations, and there are no Christians who do not need to remind themselves constantly of their obligations in this matter, and to abstain from the excuses which come so readily to the mind and tongue. For the Church of

England would not the removal from Canon Law of the anomalies here mentioned be a shining example of the 'brotherly charity' which the Canon Law itself emphatically recommends?

Synodal government of the Church of England, at national, diocesan and deanery level, was set up in 1970, not by a change in Canon Law, but by a measure which received the assent of Parliament. It marks a definite step forward in the way earlier taken by many other churches towards ascertaining and executing the will of the whole church, and not just that of the ordained priesthood; it could be said to be at least a partial recognition in constitutional terms of the priesthood of the whole church and the ministry of all Christian people.

The Church Assembly, dating from the Enabling Act of 1919, and consisting of clergy and laypeople, possessed certain powers, notably in legislative and financial matters, which it had taken over from the wholly clerical Convocations of Canterbury and York; but the Convocations still held the real power in matters which vitally affected the corporate life of the Church. Now the Synod took the place of both, except that certain residual functions were left to the Convocations.

The enthusiasm which greeted this reform concealed its defects; but these have gradually come to light. I noted with interest at the inauguration of the General Synod in 1970 the fairly large number of women members, and their greater youthfulness than that of the clergy and their male lay colleagues. But I could not fail also to suspect that many of the lay members owed their election partly to the fact that they had greater leisure for three long annual meetings of the Synod than the average layperson could contemplate. Perhaps inevitably, but certainly in fact, the Synod tends to be, and to remain, a middle-class affair, perhaps an upper-middle-class affair, and the effect of this has been frequently seen in its later deliberations. (Other churches are not much better about this.)

The division of the Synod into three houses – of bishops, clergy and laypeople – is in conformity with long-established Anglican tradition. It can be defended as providing for the clear expression of the will of the three 'estates' of the Anglican community, and as saving the vote of the bishops, who in Anglican theology represent the apostles (in a sense not, perhaps, entirely agreed upon by Anglican thinkers) and are the acknowledged leaders and teachers of the Church of England in matters spiritual and intellectual, from being swamped by the votes of the so-called 'lower clergy' and the laity. This defence will not satisfy those who hold that the government of the church should be conducted on strictly democratic principles, but the Church of England does not claim to be a democratic institution.

But the constitutional stipulation that on issues which involve a change in the life of the church a proposal must obtain a majority in each House (of a size determined by the Synod, but a two-thirds majority is usually required on 'great' matters), as well as a majority of all the votes cast, to be approved, has had some curious consequences. On a long series of proposals which could be described as 'progressive', and certainly have had an eye to the changing needs of human society in the years since the Synod first met, the voting of the Synod as a whole has given a majority in favour, but one House, the House of Clergy, has not registered a sufficient majority in favour for the proposals to go through. These proposals were concerned with the ordination of women, the right of women ordained in Anglican churches overseas to preside at the eucharist in this country and the Anglican-Methodist Scheme.

This means, in plain terms, that each House has the power of veto over the wishes of the majority of the Synod, and that the House of Clergy has exercised its veto on many occasions, and, it may safely be said, on each occasion in favour of the *status quo*. This is true even in the case of the Covenanting Proposals where the total majority, though large, was not adequate. This was because the opponents in the House of Clergy were numerous enough to offset the majorities of the other Houses in the total count.

In each of these cases the will of the bishops, the acknowledged leaders and teachers of the church, was set aside. It is a matter of history that in each case the opposition in the House of Clergy was almost entirely formed by those of the Anglo-Catholic persuasion (except that in the case of the Anglican-Methodist Scheme they were joined by a group of Evangelicals); in other words, those in the Church of England who make the highest claims in theological terms for the successors of the Apostles had no compunction about voting them down on issues of theology, pastoral ethics and Christian unity on which they could reasonably be expected to follow the episcopal – and archiepiscopal – lead.

But this evil thing, or anomaly, or statesmanlike device to allow the Almighty to overrule the majority in the interests of the wisdom which he has imparted to a particular group – according to one's point of view – is not the whole of the difficulty. The organization of Anglican churchpeople, and especially the clergy, into clearly defined parties with a stated programme actively pursued in church politics, has long been the wonder, but not the envy, of other Christians. They have been somewhat comforted on being told that the majority of Anglicans do not in fact belong to any of the parties; but they know that this fact does not affect the outcome very much.

When I was heavily involved in the formulation and consideration of the Anglican-Methodist Scheme more than a decade ago, I sometimes feared, no doubt in an unworthy spirit, that the issue would be settled not by the Synod's vote, but by 'party managers' in the corridors of power, that is, of Church House, Westminster; and indeed some of those party managers told me that it was the tripartite constitution of the General Synod which has given a considerable fillip to such machinations as these fears suggest. To sway the vote of the whole Synod, consisting of representatives from all over the country with minds of their own and a great number of conflicting interests, could prove too great a task in the time available for even the best organized party. But to do this in the small House of Clergy, to the extent of persuading more than a third to vote in a particular way, was by no means too great a task, especially since the way had usually been prepared by efficient electioneering when the Synod was elected.

Thus the wishes of those in the middle were easily overborne, though in one case at least (that of the vote about women ordained overseas) the opposition had, it seems, to make its success sure by circulating to its supporters a sheet of instructions for the debate, including one to abstain from personal abuse when speaking and to avoid going to the toilet when the vote was imminent.

All this is not to cast doubt on the sincerity of the convictions of those who opposed the 'progressive' proposals. But it does surely raise serious questions about a constitution which makes politicking so easy for those who have no scruples about indulging in it, and causes rumours, accurate or not, of manoeuvres even more outrageous than those here described, to fly around uncontrolled.

The appointment of bishops and deans by the Crown is a contentious subject so much discussed that it is not necessary to say much about it, except that it still raises considerable questions in non-Anglican minds. These questions do not spring from any jealousy of privilege, though the seating of bishops, and of the leaders of no other church, in the House of Lords (except for Donald Soper on his own merits), could be described as a refusal to employ the total available wisdom of the church in the counsels of the nation. But perhaps it is balanced by the forbidding of Anglican clergy to sit in the House of Commons. The real matters of concern are whether the Church of England is free to have as its leaders only those who are best qualified to lead it; and whether a system by which clergy owe their preferment and bishops their position to the decision of politicians who have quite other concerns than the welfare of the church, imposes restraints on the leaders of the church which a sound theology would strongly condemn.

The present system and its predecessors are sometimes defended on the ground that they have worked well enough, in spite of their obvious deficiencies. The register and record of eighteenth-century and early nineteenth-century bishops give little force to this defence. The second half of the nineteenth century, it is true, marked a considerable improvement in practice, in spite of the strictures of Anthony Trollope. The present century continued the improvement, though some would point out a preponderance of 'safe' men in episcopal office; but it has not been without its anomalies. The appointment of E. W. Barnes, a man remarkable for many intellectual gifts and much pastoral awareness, but scarcely 'episcopabilis', in the judgment even of his friends, seems to have owed more to his sympathy with the political views of the Prime Minister, Ramsay MacDonald, than to any other reason that can be discerned. The appointment of William Temple as Archbishop of Canterbury was unduly delayed by Winston Churchill's dislike of his 'socialist' leanings.

It will be rightly be pointed out that the system was recently reformed by agreement between the church and James Callaghan, then Prime Minister. In the case of an episcopal vacancy, after a considerable amount of consultation, both regional and national, within the church, and even in some cases with members of other churches (though this is not laid down), certain names for a particular appointment appear. The committee of twelve churchpeople which advises the Prime Minister chooses two and puts them in the order of its own preference. Both names go to the Prime Minister for the final choice. If there is a majority of eight to four, or a larger majority still, for one of the candidates, the Prime Minister is required either to choose him for recommendation to the Sovereign or to ask for additional names. Otherwise the Prime Minister's choice is free. Margaret Thatcher as Prime Minister was then within her rights when she recommended the present Bishop of London to the Queen; it is understood that the voting in the Committee was seven to five against him. Mrs Thatcher's motives are not open to public scrutiny. But the conjecture that her choice was not entirely un-political cannot be completely discounted. Certainly it is entertained by many people. The See of London is, after those of Canterbury and York, the most important and influential See in England. Is there a credible defence of this method of appointing its holder, or the holder of any other See?

The matters raised in this chapter are not the concern of the Church of England alone. While that church claims to be the 'church of the land' they are the concerns of all, and especially of all Christians. But the first thing about them is that they hamper the work of the Church of England.

3

The Low Standing of Women

It is ironic that the Supreme Governor of the Church of England is a woman; that the officer of state who at present recommends to the Supreme Governor those who are to be bishops and deans in that church is a woman; and that elsewhere in that church no woman is entitled to hold any position of power or authority in which she can shape, or help to shape, the life of the church as a whole.

This does not mean, of course, that women do not exercise any spiritual or intellectual authority in the Church of England. The reverse is the case. There are women with spiritual and intellectual gifts who profoundly influence the life and thought of Anglican groups, Anglican parishes, and individual Anglicans of both sexes; and in many cases their influence spreads far beyond the bounds of their own denomination. Women in Religious Orders, by their manner of life, their teaching, and their service to the under-privileged, are for ever maintaining the inner strength of Christian communities; deaconesses, accredited women lay workers and readers share the pastoral and preaching work of the clergy in a distinctive way now recognized as essential by clergy and lay-people alike. Moreover, women hold important administrative positions up to the rank of a Church Commissioner and the Chair-person of the Board for Mission and Unity (though no woman has yet been appointed as the Secretary of any Board of the General

34

Synod). There is a woman on the teaching staff of each theological college, and women teach in every capacity throughout the whole educational enterprise of the church. Women theologians and women writers and speakers on theological subjects receive the same respect as men. Much of this indicates a considerable change in recent years.

Yet we are still on the fringe of the subject when we state or acknowledge these facts. It is important that this should be seen to be the case, lest anyone should suppose that now that women are to be found in the positions listed above, all that women can legitimately claim has been granted, and no more attention needs to be given to the matter. The real situation is that the Church of England furnishes a clear example of the acceptance by Christian churches of the institutional models of society at large. These models until recently excluded women altogether from positions of authority; now they have been modified by giving some important jobs to 'token' women. The Church of England has done a little better than mere tokenism, and there are signs of hope that it will do better still. But at present the similarity to the models of society remains, and any attempt to advance the cause of women brings out the fierce opposition of those entrenched in power.[1]

There are probably, for reasons deep in English religious and social history, far more Anglican women, in proportion to the total membership of their church, of outstanding ability and a high degree of educational attainment, and of considerable ability and better than average education, than in any other church in this country. It is extremely likely that within the next decade or so there will be at least as many women as men who fall within these two categories within the membership of the Church of England. Yet, even if for the moment we leave the priesthood on one side, the proportion of women to men in positions of responsibility is pitifully small; and the inveterate tendency to allocate the jobs of minor importance to women and those of major importance to men – except, of course, when there are no men available – though it has decreased at the higher levels of the church, is still inordinately strong at every other level.

35

This is not the result of mere constitutional anomalies, now recognized as such, but because of the slowness of constitutional change in the Church of England, likely to be steadily, but not hastily, amended. Rather, it expresses a dominant, widespread and deeply rooted attitude of mind among the clergy and (to a lesser extent) the laity of that church. Evidence for an attitude of mind is, no doubt, difficult to collect and assess, since few people nowadays are willing to confess openly to a belief in the inferiority of women, and the many Anglicans who hold this belief try to conceal it by such phrases as: 'I am a great believer in the equality of the sexes, but . . .' But they do not conceal it successfully. It comes out in insufferably patronizing remarks made to women and about women (of which I have heard many in meetings of clergy in which it has been my duty, and very often my pleasure, to be present), in the quiet sidetracking of projects in which women would bear an equal responsibility with men, pained comments about certain 'militant' women, and a multiplicity of snide jokes (the most offensive being reserved for all-male assemblies and private conversations), such as the recent remark of a diocesan bishop in a diocesan synod, on the subject of the 'Movement for the Ordination of Women', to the effect that he would find it difficult to be associated with an organization the initials of whose title rhymed with 'cow'.

It is not to be claimed, of course, that the Church of England is alone in this attitude to women, and alone in the possession of a constitution which makes it hard for a woman to be given great responsibility. This is a malaise with which all the Christian bodies in this country, except for the Society of Friends, have been infected in the past and to some extent are still infected. Traditional ways of thinking about women, and interpretations of the Bible tailored to suit these traditional ways of thinking, have laid a very heavy hand on all the English churches, which they have all been slow to shake off. Baptists, both the Congregational and the Presbyterian constituents of the United Reformed Churches, and not least the Methodists, are bound in all honesty to admit that they have adjusted themselves only slowly to the belated rediscovery that God created both male and female in his own image and that St Paul's statement that in Christ there is neither male nor female can no longer be explained away. There are groups of people in all the Free Churches (including women who have persuaded their churches to recognize and appreciate their gifts and have 'made it' to the top) to whom feminism, even of the Christian sort, is a dirty word. Nor can the Free Churches claim to have understood to the full the radical changes involved in opening all doors to women. But if there were to be an order of merit based on the recognition of the equal valuation of women with men in the Christian community and in Christian understanding, the Church of England would occupy a very lowly place in it – slightly above the Roman Catholic Church and the Orthodox Churches.[2]

Oppressed by this situation in general, and often affronted by the particular treatment of themselves (unseemly treatment for which it is, alas, possible to furnish a great deal of evidence), many of the more gifted daughters of the Church of England have either left the church altogether or have found a way to use their gifts for the good of their fellows and the glory of God in extraecclesiastical ways while not actually renouncing their membership of the church. The number of these is steadily growing, and surely must be a matter of great concern to everyone who is not a male chauvinist. Of course there are many activities outside the church in which the gifts of Christians are urgently needed; but the repudiation by the church, at a time when, surely, all its resources are needed, of something like half of its potential wealth in terms of persons and their personal contributions, is surely inexcusable.

Those who believe that Victorian piety is the right kind of piety for our age also, will say in answer to this that women should wait in docility and humility until the church in its wisdom puts matters right, meanwhile praying, no doubt, and working in a modest way, for this to happen. But when patience, docility and humility have so patently failed to make any impression on those who have the power to effect change but do not wish to do so, and when they have given no effective assistance to those – and they are many, and they include a large number of men in the priesthood and outside it – who desire change, it is time to ask whether these three Christian virtues have been rightly understood in this context. Humility is the recognition of oneself as one truly is, not self-denigration or the tacit acceptance of denigration by others. Patience is the power to endure for oneself such denigration and other pain until the truth eventually comes through, but not to endure it for others regardless of the injustice that is being done. Docility is the willingness to learn from those wiser than oneself, but not from those whose teaching rests on foundations which one no longer accepts. And if evil is to be defeated, to humility, patience and docility must be added courage and faith.

We are nearest to the crux of the whole matter if we reflect on the refusal of the Church of England to ordain women as priests. There are at present many – *how* many, no one knows; but the exact number is not important – communicant and devoted women members of the Church of England who are deeply convinced that they are called by God to the priesthood, and who, at least to any human observer, possess the gifts and graces needed for the exercise of a priestly, pastoral, teaching and preaching ministry. If it is asked how such a fact can be known to someone who is not a bishop and not even an Anglican, the answer is that he has been approached for counsel, in deep concern about the church and their own vocation, by several women of whom this is true, and that he knows many wholly responsible people of sound judgment, Anglicans and others, who have been similarly approached. He knows from many conversations that this is not a matter of the rights of women (though for the moralist and the theologian this question also is involved); it is a matter of the call of God, the empowerment of the Spirit and the ministry of the church. He is well aware that a personal claim to be called by God is not in itself a proof that God is calling; any such claim has to be verified by the church – as indeed is the practice in all churches which ordain women, in relation to both men and women.

So far as qualifications for the ordained ministry are concerned, their presence is scarcely deniable in many of the people about whom we are now thinking; and when it is observed, as it must be and is, that some of those already ordained, men who are perfectly acceptable as priests, do not possess those qualities to as high a degree as the women whom the Church of England refuses to ordain, we are forced to the bizarre conclusion that in the official thinking of that church any man who possesses the minimum qualifications for the priesthood has an eligibility for ordination which no woman, however high her qualifications, has; in other words, that a basic qualification for priesthood is, simply and solely, sex – and biological sex at that.

The absurdity of this situation reaches a climax when women who have been trained in theological colleges precisely as male ordinands are trained are told that they are not suitable for ordination, while their male colleagues go off to be ordained deacons, priests, and possibly in due course bishops. Perhaps the women should have been trained in a ladies' seminary where their 'feminine' qualities are developed and their 'masculine' qualities suppressed.

At this point it has to be added, without any trace of sentimentality, but as a sober fact of contemporary Christian experience, that in many, perhaps all, cases, women who in spite of their deep sense of vocation have been rejected for the priesthood, are deeply humiliated and frustrated in their innermost being. They do not, of course, reveal this humiliation and frustration, except very rarely, in public addresses or conversation, partly because of the scornful rejoinder which they justifiably expect to receive from some of their hearers, but the distress is none the less real for that. And there is good reason for saying that the rejection of the Covenanting Proposals by the General Synod, partly at least on the ground that their approval would have meant the acceptance of the ordained women of the Free Churches,[3] has injected salt into an already painful wound.

All the elements of this chapter so far, surely, add up to a general situation which demands scrutiny of the most careful and thoroughgoing kind. Probably the best starting point for such a scrutiny is precisely the question of women's ordination, since it attracts to itself so many of the issues raised by the theology of the ministry of women, and its resolution would make the resolution of other problems much simpler. Indeed it raises fundamental questions about the nature of God, the nature of humankind and the nature of the church.

The controversy about women priests has for the most part been conducted on the assumption that the onus of proof is on those who maintain that women ought to be eligible for ordination: the ground for this assumption being that the church in general has not ordained women until very recent times, and that the non-ordination of women is therefore part of established tradition.

But the assumption needs to be questioned. No one would now say that in the matter of slavery the onus of proof was on those who wished to abolish it. It is nearer the truth to say that the defenders of the *status quo*, in order to defend the *status quo* and their own interests, tried hard to put the onus on its attackers; whereas, in fact, on grounds of basic Christian doctrine, anyone who kept slaves, or upheld the institution of slavery, had to build a great edifice of proof if he was to justify his position.

We can see this now by hindsight. And we can see the same in respect of many other 'reforms', such as the extension of the franchise and the provision of universal education. So it is, and should be seen to be, in the present case. It can be positively stated that since in baptism and the other sacraments of the church (apart from ordination) no distinction is or can be made between men and women, those who wish to make it in the matter of ordination must accept the burden of proof if they are to establish their case; otherwise it simply goes by default.

This is a 'hard saying' for some, although the General Synod of the Church of England may have accepted it, at least temporarily, when it resolved in 1975 that there were no fundamental objections to the ordination of women to the priesthood; and to insist on it here might alienate those who would on other grounds support such ordination. Without any assumption, therefore, as to where the burden of proof lies, the arguments on each side will be set out with comments. On both sides the arguments which involved theological principles must, of course, have pride of place, although they have not always done so in recent discussions.

Some of those urged against the ordination of women seem to depend on the notion of God the Father as male, in the form of saying: 'God the Father is male, Jesus Christ his Son is male (the sex of the Holy Spirit is not specified), therefore the priest, representing the role of the Father in the Trinity and the maleness of Christ, must be male.' But to ascribe sex to the First Person of the Trinity (no doubt in a highly spiritualized form, and on the ground that Jesus habitually addressed God as 'Father') is so unacceptably anthropomorphic that serious theologians do not usually bring this consideration into the discussion – except that some Orthodox theologians in spite of their strong doctrine of the feminine in the Trinity do sometimes lay stress upon it.

The argument from the maleness of *Christ* has usually dominated the discussion and has to be reckoned with. It is stated forcibly thus by E. L. Mascall:

In the strict and proper sense, the only ontologically original and ultimate priesthood is that of Christ; it is identical with his status as Son, Word and Apostle of the eternal Father. This priesthood subsists in eternity and it enters into the created world in his assumption of human nature in the womb of Mary. The Church, consisting of those men and women who are incorporated into him, is his Body and his Bride. The Church is taken into his priesthood ... Priesthood belongs to Christ as the *Son* of the Eternal Father. He became man as male, not by accident but because he is Son and not Daughter; because what was to be communicated to the created world in human form in the incarnation was the relation which he has to the Father. The fact that he has only one sex, and that the male, does not make his humanity incomplete. Humanity belongs to him fully in the mode of masculinity; he does not need to be a hermaphrodite in order to be fully human, any more than he needs to be a eunuch to avoid favouring one sex over the other. And because the ordained priest is not exercising a priesthood of his own but is the agent and instrument through which Christ is exercising *his* priesthood, he too must be male. To say that 'the Church has restricted the priesthood to males' is to speak in far too negative a manner; rather, Christ exercises his priesthood in the Church through human beings who possess human nature in the same sexual mode in which he possesses it.[4]

The only comment on this required at this point is that it is possible to accept all the premisses of Mascall relating to the incarnation of Christ, up to the point of agreeing that 'humanity belongs to him fully in the mode of masculinity', and then to draw a conclusion from them which is exactly opposite to his – as we shall see.

A statement of what is virtually the same argument as Mascall's is made in the same book by Kallistos Ware, an English Orthodox theologian. His use of the Orthodox conception of an icon, as 'making present a spiritual reality that surpasses it, but of which it acts as the sign', makes his writing on the subject particularly attractive to English Christians who know that we have much to learn from the Orthodox.

Ware argues that the 'ministerial priest' is 'an icon of the unique high priest Christ'; and because Christ is *man* and not woman, this priest must be male. All Christians, male and female, share the *royal* priesthood of the whole people of God; the *ministerial* priesthood, which is distinct from the royal priesthood, is open to men only. The priest, as icon, does not remind us of, or represent, an absent Christ; he makes Christ present; and only a man can do this.[5]

Once again, it may be commented, the key premiss is impeccable. There is no need to belong to an especially 'high' school of Catholic theology, or to the Orthodox tradition, to believe that the ministerial priest is an 'icon' of Christ in the Orthodox sense of icon. The concept is acceptable to many other schools of thought. And even those who hold that Ware makes too sharp a distinction between 'royal' and 'ministerial' priesthood may, indeed, find the 'icon' concept helpful. But, once again, a quite different conclusion may follow from the premiss, as we shall see.

An argument from scripture is sometimes used. 'The apostles without exception were male; therefore their successors must be male.' But in the social conditions of the time it is hard to see how

Jesus could have chosen women as apostles. And though no women were apostles, the first witnesses to the resurrection were women (Luke 24.10: John 20.15). But the chief comment must be that all the apostles were of Jewish race as well as male; it has never been held to follow that all their successors must be of Jewish race. 'Ah, but', it has been said, 'sex is not comparable with race in this regard: it constitutes a different kind of differentia between people.' But this reply is a neat example of the fallacy of *petitio principii*, that is, of assuming what has to be proved. The very point at issue is whether sex *does* constitute a unique differentia.

Of more weight is an argument from tradition. It runs like this: the Holy Spirit guides the church into all the truth. The truth referred to is the truth that is in Christ, and the guidance of the Spirit is the unfolding of that truth during the centuries which have followed the incarnation. It is embodied in the 'tradition of the church'. Now in the undivided church of the first ten centuries and in the churches of the East and the West which arose from the separation of Rome and Constantinople in the eleventh century, the tradition that only men may be ordained as priests has been unfalteringly maintained by theologians, lawyers and administrators alike. The same is true of the Church of England since its break with Rome in the sixteenth century. The ordination of women is therefore contrary to unbroken tradition.

About this it must be said that it assumes a definition of tradition which is over-narrow in two important respects. On this definition tradition is (a) limited to certain parts of Christendom, as though the Holy Spirit had withheld his guidance from the rest; (b) restricted to the past in such a way that no change in circumstances or development of spiritual insight can modify any of its deliverances. This is traditionalist fundamentalism of a most rigid sort, characteristic of Western Christendom much more than of the East, and if it were correct all Christians would be tied down in theory to many beliefs and practices which they have in practice abandoned, for instance to certain views of the nature of scripture unquestioned until the rise of biblical scholarship, but now untenable, and to certain views about soul and body which virtually all modern scholars regard as unscriptural. Without any disrespect to the guidance of the Holy Spirit, indeed with a much greater respect for it, a wider, deeper and more dynamic theology of tradition is required. The argument is in any case eroded by the fact that many churches in the Anglican Communion – churches which presumably inherit and highly value the tradition – do in fact ordain women as priests. They have come to see, no doubt, that the refusal to do so is based on non-biblical, mediaeval anthropology which sees woman as a defective male.

Related to the argument from tradition is the 'ecumenical' argument, which indeed is the one that seems to have exercised the greatest influence in recent years. Here it is. The Roman Catholic Church does not ordain women, and has no intention of doing so. The Orthodox Churches do not ordain women and will never do so. If the Church of England were to ordain women, all hope of reunion with Rome or the Orthodox Churches would be destroyed.

This argument, of course, is not really ecumenical. Ecumenism is concerned with the whole church in the whole world, and invites each part of the church to contribute its insights to the treasury of the whole, even when they run counter to the insights of other parts of the church; and furnishes a forum in which conflicting insights may be studied afresh and reconciliation sought. On this very matter of the ordination of women the WCC Faith and Order Commission, in the Study on the Community of Women and Men in the Church, has produced *The Ordination of Women in Ecumenical Perspective*; and the notable Faith and Order report on *Baptism, Eucharist and Ministry* (1982) has a very carefully balanced section on the subject.

On the particular, and local, issue of the possible endangering of relations between the Church of England and the Roman Catholic Church if the Church of England ordains women, it has to be pointed out that the Roman Catholic Church is concerned with relations between itself and the Anglican Communion, not specifically the Church of England; and, since several churches within that communion already ordain women, the difficulty which is feared already exists, and would not be increased if the

Church of England followed the example of its sister churches in the USA and elsewhere. In any case certain Roman Catholic theologians[6] already favour the ordination of women, and there is no built-in reason why the teaching of the church should not in due course follow their lead.

The Orthodox Churches have indeed set their faces, in an apparently indomitable manner, against the ordination of women as priests. But so many years will pass before there is any question of visible unity between them and the Church of England that it is even possible that their mind may change before that question becomes insistent.

And let this question be firmly put: are not the relations of the Church of England with the Free Churches who share its mission to this country equally important? From some Anglican conversations, and some debates in the General Synod, one might conclude that they do not matter at all.

There is an argument from the 'other ministries' which women already fulfill or may well come to fulfill. The Archbishop of Canterbury, addressing the World Council of Churches' Consultation on 'the Community of Women and Men in the Church' in Sheffield in the summer of 1981, acknowledged that the ordained ministry is a masculine status organization, and urged the women in his audience, instead of setting their hearts on joining such an institution – though he could see no theological objection to their doing so – to apply their gifts and sensitivities to ministries which did not need ordination where they would be particularly valuable – for example, to medical work, and to counselling and the distressed, especially prisoners, prostitutes and homosexuals.[7]

It was not quite clear to those who heard his address whether Dr Runcie would, in the last resort, oppose the ordination of women on some non-theological principle. But his words were certainly taken by some to mean that there are different ministries for men and women, and those suitable for women do not include ordination to the priesthood. But surely the spiritual sensitivity which he ascribed to women (and not, apparently, to men) is invaluable *within* the priesthood – as well as in the ministries of laypeople. Indeed its absence – if it *be* absent, and certainly not all male priests possess it – is a very serious defect in the Anglican priesthood as it is at present constituted. And the fact that women can fulfil many ministries outside the priesthood is a very feeble argument for not allowing them to exercise their gifts within it. The same, exactly, could be said about men.

Arguments have been brought forward from time to time from female psychology – that women, for example, become too personally involved in the troubles of individual people, that they attend too much to detail instead of to general issues, that they find it hard to make decisions on their own, that they become 'bossy' when given authority, and, quite baldly, that they are emotional while men are rational.[8] It is certainly improper and dangerous to generalize about whole sexes in this way, and these very statements could in any case be slightly modified to indicate that women are more compassionate, more conscientious and practical, more willing to consult others, more willing to take the lead when given a chance, and less doctrinaire, than men. But in fact, while certain general sexual characteristics may perhaps be discerned, no one yet knows how many of them are genetic and how many are historically and socially caused; it seems that nearly everyone is a mixture of so-called male and female characteristics.

So this argument is wholly inconclusive in itself, and its significance, if any, is annulled by the experience of those churches in which women are ordained. No harm either to church or persons has been recorded – though of course some women are psychologically unsuitable for priesthood and some of these may have been wrongly ordained; this has always applied in the case of some men – and the ministries of these churches are steadily being enhanced by the greater variety of spiritual, intellectual *and* emotional insights that they can now call upon.[9] As a Methodist minister, I can testify to the positive gain of women's colleagueship and understanding.

These, then, are the arguments against 'women priests', and what needs to be said about them. The arguments on the other side are simple, straightforward and fundamental, though they also require some comment.

In the first place, the gospel, as recorded in the New Testament and embodied in Jesus, offers salvation and wholeness to all people without any discrimination or inequality of any kind. All who believe are children of God. The church, and its sacraments and liturgy and care, are open to all. In Christ there is neither male nor female (just as there is neither Jew nor Gentile, neither slave nor free); they are one person in him.

Within the church the Spirit gives diverse gifts to individual people, and has so ordered the affairs of the church that some with particular gifts are called to the ministry which is conferred by ordination. There is no hint in any of the descriptions in the New Testament of these diverse ministries that any of them are limited to one sex or race or class. To introduce such limits is wholly alien to the spirit and content of the gospel.

Here some comments are needed. There *are* Pauline passages in which it is said that man is the head of woman (I Cor. 11.3), and one famous sentence in which Paul orders the women to be silent in the churches (I Cor. 14.34). And this indeed could be said to be the tenor of several other passages. Taken literally, these passages rule out women readers and preachers as well as woman priests – and a good deal more besides.

But Paul did not obey his own instructions, for he did not forbid the four daughters of Philip the Evangelist to exercise their prophetic gifts (Acts 21.9); he encouraged Phoebe to hold office in Cenchreae (Rom. 16.1), and probably other women to do the same elsewhere. Perhaps he changed his mind? But it is true that no women were apostles, and probable that no women were appointed to the office of presbyter/bishop in New Testament times.

We have then an inconsistency between the basic principles of Paul's gospel on the one hand, and his views on church order and the relations between men and women on the other.

This is not the only example of such inconsistency in Paul. He is similarly inconsistent in the matters of slavery (Col. 3.22) and obedience to the civil power (Rom. 13.1). It is catholic wisdom through the ages to insist on the fundamental principles of the gospel; and to regard views and practices inconsistent with them, even when they are found in the New Testament, as a part of the inheritance from the past which has not yet been subjected to the full light of the gospel. This the church has constantly felt free, and indeed guided, to do.

The second theological argument starts from agreement with those who take the other side of the case, that the ordained priest represents, is the icon of, the Great High Priest, Jesus Christ. But it draws a different conclusion: the Great High Priest is not the *incarnate* Christ, who was undoubtedly male, Jewish and a man of the first century, but the *ascended and glorified* Christ, in whom all the high potentialities of humankind, male and female, are taken up, fulfilled and transcended; *this* is the High Priest who 'has taken his seat at the right hand of the throne of Majesty in the Heavens' (Heb. 8.1;). This High Priest, the glorified Son, the Word of the Father, is to be represented on earth by men *and* women; the representation by men only is incomplete.

Now the ordained priest represents not only God in Christ to humankind, but also humankind to God. This representation also is surely incomplete if it is made by men only or by women only; it is only a whole priesthood, of men and women, that can represent humankind in its fullness.

We do not exaggerate if we say that to ascribe sex to the Great High Priest goes near to the verge of heresy, and perhaps beyond it. To deny womanhood the role of representing, along with manhood, both the Great High Priest and humankind, is to condemn the church to a defective priesthood.

It will perhaps be urged, in favour of a sexually differentiated Great High Priest, and hence an exclusively male priesthood, that in Hebrews 7.28 the author says that the Great High Priest 'appointed by the words of the oath which supersedes the Law, is the Son, made perfect for ever'. None of the Fathers, however, when they speak of the divine Son, has any thought of ascribing a male character to him; such ascription is modern, perhaps engendered by the present controversy. The Fathers in passage after passage are interested in the *humanity* of the Son, the Logos, and make no reference to maleness, lest they suggest that the divine essence is male; for Christ, the Logos, the Son, they insist, with the Creed, is of the same essence with the Father.[10]

The third theological argument, from tradition, draws attention to the fact that, even in the narrow and static sense in which it is used by the opponents of women's ordination, 'the tradition' is not unanimous in insisting on male headship in the church; for instance, many mediaeval abbesses in this country exercised authority over priests, and in Spain the Cistercian Abbesses of Las Huelgas had spiritual and temporal jurisdiction over the clergy of sixty-four villages until 1874. But it is true that in 'the tradition' as so far defined the right to preside at the eucharist has been withheld from women.

But if we see 'tradition' in the wider, and dynamic, sense of the Spirit's guidance of the whole church, and of guidance which is still bringing new truths to light as the whole truth which is in Christ is progressively unfolded, then we shall find that in that tradition women have been ordained to the full ministry of word and sacraments in several of the churches of the Reformation, and in several Anglican Churches, more especially in the present century; and we shall see here yet one more example of a prophetic insight, which, first granted in a particular part of the Church Catholic, spreads steadily throughout the whole. A very notable example of this is the modern understanding of the Bible; the admission of women to the priesthood is indeed, among other things, a direct consequence of that.

The open-minded reader will make up his or her own mind about the relative strengths of the arguments for and against the ordination of women as priests. It will perhaps be evident from my comments on these arguments that I find those against such ordination very unconvincing. In fact, I regard them as so weak that I am forced to suppose that those who offer or support them have other and deeper, unspoken, reasons for their point of view; and to ask certain very serious questions.

Is it not the case that many of the bishops, clergy and laypeople who vote against the ordination of women as priests, and even against the celebration of the eucharist by women duly ordained overseas into the Anglican priesthood, are traditionalists in a bad and not a good sense – in the unhealthy sense of preserving the past because it is the past, and because they feel more secure in the past than in the present? Such traditionalists have, historically, defended in turn the harassment of Jews, Dissenters and Roman Catholics, the institution of slavery, the subordination of the working classes, white supremacy, Anglican supremacy, and now male supremacy, and will no doubt maintain this present attitude until the consensus of Christendom finally brings them to a different point of view.

Is it not the case that the opposition to women priests springs partly, and in some cases chiefly, from antique and deeply-rooted notions about the evil of sexuality, and of women as its embodiment, and about women as defective men; and from an atavistic dread of the dark mystery of womanhood now (as they fear) threatening to overwhelm and take over church and society?

Is it not the case that until the people of whom we are speaking come to terms with sexuality, their own and that of others, and recognize it as a gift of God with immense potentiality, no doubt for evil, but also for good in the enhancement of human life, the Church of England will be crippled in its endeavour to bring guidance, hope and love into the relationships of men and women and into family life in our day?

Is it not the case that while the present situation remains disregarded and untreated in spite of the enlightenment shared by many Anglicans with many of their fellow Christians, the Church of England will continue to treat women as second class members of their own church, as well as denying them ordination to the priesthood?

Yet a more hopeful question can also perhaps be posed: Free Church women ministers when they were ordained inevitably entered the ordained ministry of their churches *as it then was* with its male-oriented procedures and conventions. Their presence in that ministry is bound in due course to change, diversify and enhance its character, but this will take time. Anglican women who believe themselves to be divinely called to ordination are still engaged in the struggle for acceptance, and many of them as they look at the Anglican priesthood and its response to their arguments are coming to ask if they really wish to enter that ministry *as it now is*. Many of them are saying that they emphatically do not, that what they have in mind is a new, whole, enriched ministry which could change the shape of the church and deepen its understanding of the nature and being of God, and that they believe that women have an indispensable contribution to make in that regard. Surely the Church of England will soon take serious notice of these convictions and put them to the test? And if it does, will it not find itself impelled towards not only the ordination of women but also to the renewal of the priesthood?

4

The Dilemma of Establishment

On a recent BBC programme celebrating the first thirty years of the reign of Queen Elizabeth II there was no allusion at all to anything that the Queen had done for the Church of England of which she is the Supreme Governor, although there were some shots of Westminster Abbey on ceremonial occasions. The omission may have been due to forgetfulness or carelessness on the part of the BBC; or to its belief that the public had no interest in the relations between the Church of England and the Crown. It certainly does not reflect the attitude of the Queen herself, for she takes her ecclesiastical responsibilities very seriously, and does not regard Westminster Abbey or St Paul's Cathedral simply as convenient locations for state events. The Church of England, by law established, is one of her deepest concerns. But what does 'by law established' mean?

Some important elements in the complex phenomenon which is known as 'the Establishment' have already come to our attention in the course of this book – the appointment of bishops and deans by the Crown, for instance, and the remote control of Anglican worship by the Crown in Parliament. There are many others, not all of them important, but helping to complete the pattern. The Archbishop of Canterbury, appointed by the Sovereign on the advice of the Prime Minister, after consultation within the church, has precedence in honour over all peers of the realm.

With the assistance of some of his fellow bishops, but of no one from any other church in any significant capacity, he crowns the Sovereign. Twenty-six bishops, and no one from any other church as of right, sit in the House of Lords; Lord Soper, a Methodist minister, sits there simply as a leading socialist, and it has occurred to no government to introduce legislation for the nomination of a Roman Catholic bishop or a Free Church minister to sit with the Anglican bishops. It is the privilege of the Church of England to hold the official service on the anniversary of the Sovereign's accession (rarely held), and on all other national occasions, and it has no obligation to invite the participation of any other church.

The Church of England, as entitled by the law of the land, owns the cathedrals, the parish churches and the parsonages of England, together with much other property and an estimated revenue of £80,000,000. The property and revenue are administered by the Church Commissioners for England, a body formed by the fusion in 1948 of the Ecclesiastical Commissioners, which from 1835 to 1948 had the sole power to hold and purchase land for the church; and Queen Anne's Bounty, a body formed in 1704 when Queen Anne handed over to the Church of England the money confiscated from the church by Henry VIII, and directed that it should be used to increase the income of the poorer clergy. The Church Commissioners consist of the archbishops and bishops, three lay Church Estates Commissioners, twenty-five persons, clerical and lay, appointed by the General Synod, four laypersons appointed by the Crown and four by the Archbishop of Canterbury, some state officials, and, for good measure, representatives of the cities of London and York and the Universities of Oxford and Cambridge. All, of course, are Anglicans. The main work is carried out by a board of governors, not more than thirty strong. The Commissioners are not answerable to the General Synod of the church, although they are required to make recommendations to Parliament through the Synod on statutory fees for marriages and funerals. They thus form a powerful property-owning corporation which is under no kind of democratic control within the church whose property they administer.

The Church Commissioners have the duty to pay the stipends of the clergy so far as they are able. Whereas in the past a very large proportion of such stipends came from the Commissioners, only 53% of what is needed is now available from this source. Most of the rest comes from the free-will offerings of the congregations; but even in modern conditions, which may indeed become yet more stringent, Anglican clergy and congregations have an immense financial advantage over their Roman Catholic and Free Church counterparts, who have to rely on the generosity of their people up to a point very near 100% of the stipends paid.

All archbishops and bishops (diocesan, assistant and suffragan) when their election is confirmed, all priests and deacons at their ordination, institution to any benefice, or licensing to any perpetual curacy, lectureship or preachership, must take and subscribe an Oath of Allegiance in a prescribed form to the Queen, her heirs and successors (Canon C13). Once the person concerned is instituted to a benefice, he enters on the 'parson's freehold'. The 'freehold' is not mentioned in Canon Law, but it is not thereby robbed of its potency. A clergyman cannot be deprived of his freehold while he is able and willing to perform the minimum duties, of saying Morning and Evening Prayer and celebrating Holy Communion with due regularity, preaching (or causing to be preached) at least one sermon each Sunday, performing certain teaching and pastoral duties, consulting with the parochial church council and living in the parsonage (or within three miles of his parish church if there is none) – except in cases of grave scandal, disciplinary or doctrinal. When such cases do not involve doctrine, ritual or ceremonial, they are dealt with in the church's own courts. When they do, they come in the first instance before a court established in 1963 called the Court of Ecclesiastical Causes Reserved (consisting of five judges, two of whom must be confirmed Anglicans, and three bishops); and on appeal, to a Royal Commission consisting of three Lords of Appeal and two bishops. Needless to say the processes in all cases are exceedingly long and complex; but their very complexity shows how closely the laws of the church and those of the state are intertwined. It is not surprising that each diocese has at its service a body of professional legal advisers, headed by a Chancellor, who is required to be a lawyer of high standing.

Lurking in the background, and sometimes obtruding itself into the foreground, of every clergyman's life is the system of patronage. This is a persistent relic of the Middle Ages rather than an integral part of the Establishment. Yet it fits in well with the Establishment. It has been modified and reformed from time to time, not least in recent decades, but it remains remarkably similar to what it has always been.

Under the system, no clergyman can be instituted or inducted into a living unless he has been presented to it by the patron of that living. The patron may be the Crown, the Lord Chancellor, the bishop (as is the case in about half the parishes, either absolutely or on alternate occasions), a cathedral dean and chapter, a college in Oxford or Cambridge, a trust which may be in possession of a number of benefices, or an individual person. Normally, if in any of these cases the churchwardens are unwilling to accept the person presented, or if the bishop indicates his unwillingness to induct, the patron produces another name – and, presumably, another and another, until the parties concerned are satisfied. Some of the trusts just referred to have been formed with the express purpose of acquiring the rights of patronage in certain parishes, and thus the power to introduce into these parishes only those clergymen who belong to a particular school of theological thought within the church. It is not supposed that other patrons are moved by such considerations; rather, they regard it as important to consult the wishes of the members of the parish, even if they cannot always provide exactly the man who satisfies all possible requirements.

So much for the structure of the church itself. It is often thought that since the civil disabilities of Roman Catholics, Nonconformists and Methodists have now been removed, all posts in every walk of life outside the Church of England are equally open to members of all denominations and of none. This is not quite the case. All purely 'secular' posts are indeed open to all. But there are still some denominational restrictions within the religious section of the armed forces and within the ancient universities. The Chaplain General of the forces must always be an Anglican.

Certain college headships, certain theological professorships, and all college chaplaincies are limited to Anglicans – with the corollary that worship in all college chapels is exclusively Anglican (and the anomaly that in Balliol College, Oxford, for instance, the Master, whatever his religious beliefs, if any, is Ordinary of the College Chapel). And anyone who scans the advertisement pages in *The Times Educational Supplement* for a post in Religious Studies (or their equivalent) will discover how many such posts are only for communicant members of the Church of England. The situation in these matters has been greatly eased in the last twenty-five years, but considerable obstacles to career advancement still remain; the incentive to conform to the Church of England for the sake of a job, or for the sake of prestige, is not so strong as it was, but it remains.

This then is the Establishment in its outward manifestation – a majestic and formidable edifice, with its foundations deep in the soil of English history. It is urged by some that 'the outward trappings remain whilst the inward substance is almost gone';[1] and it is true that it is sometimes hard to discover much correlation between the stately form and the reality. It was certainly right that at the Coronation the crown should be placed on the head of the Sovereign by the Archbishop of Canterbury, but not entirely realistic for the whole occasion to be conducted by the bishops and the peers of the realm, when the real power behind the throne resides in the Government and the House of Commons, whose members sat demurely in the congregation. And surely it was not appropriate that on the occasion of thanksgiving for twenty-five years of the Queen's reign the whole service in St Paul's Cathedral should be in the hands of Anglican clergymen, as if the Queen had been supported in her arduous tasks by the prayers of Anglicans alone, or that only Anglicans wished to thank God for the benefits of her reign. This was unreality carried to the point of absurdity, and involved the humiliation of many of her Majesty's subjects. But enough substance remains in the Establishment to exercise a profound influence on the policies of the Church of England and the lives of all English Christians, non-Anglicans as well as Anglicans.

Free Church people, whatever they may have thought in the past, can understand why many Anglicans wish the Establishment to be retained in roughly its present form, although they suppose that no one in his senses would wish to conserve its every particularity. Several arguments can be adduced for its continuance. It can be plausibly defended as a national institution which, for all its inconsistencies and compromises, or indeed because of them, works. It has been created and developed by long religious and political experience, and to abolish it would be to cancel the wisdom of our forefathers in the interest of contemporary trends of thought. This is a characteristically Anglican argument, of course, and can always be used to justify the *status quo* on any matter, but it has a certain cogency in matters of religion, where the past is always relevant to the issues of the present. As was agreed by the Anglican–Methodist Unity Commission in 1968, and not questioned in the debates which followed in either church:

> The Church of England is 'by law established'. Its partnership with the state is part of England's history. This partnership has never had a written basis, and does not depend on a theory, Hooker's or any other, for its existence; it is a fact belonging to the givenness of English life. At the present time, the partnership is sustained (so we judge) by an inarticulate but definite wish on the part of the community as a whole that England should remain a Christian country, with its government, law and education resting on Christian principles.[2]

Another argument rests on the 'Englishness' of the Church of England. As the Bishop of Bristol, John Tinsley, pointed out in a notable address to his diocesan synod in 1976, English religion is characterized by a desire to avoid extremes of doctrine or practice, by a refusal to be carried up into lengthy and complex discussion of theological matters, and by an insistence on the pragmatic and ethical nature of Christianity as it ought to be understood. These characteristics are rightly and properly embodied in a national church; and since the Church of England does indeed embody them it is admirably fitted to be the national church in this country.

This argument is not, strictly, an argument for Establishment as such, but only for a national church, and for the Church of England as the national church for us. And there will be many in the Church of England who find the argument distasteful because it makes so much of the non-dogmatic nature of Anglicanism. Yet it stands in some strength, since we actually have an established church, and Establishment may well be the best way of guaranteeing the continuance of a *national* church of the kind that England seems to need. So why destroy the existing arrangement?

The defenders of the Establishment can indeed go further than anything so far adduced, and claim that the Church of England acts as the moral guide of the nation, and of Parliament in particular, and that only an established church can act in this capacity, because only an established church has an acknowledged right to speak. This claim is perhaps symbolized by the offering of Anglican prayer on parliamentary, judicial and civic occasions. The English people as a whole cannot be thought of at present as exhibiting a very keen awareness of Christian morality in matters too numerous to be mentioned, and shows no great ethical superiority to peoples which do not possess an established church. But it is a fact that no English educator, administrator or responsible politician can speak or act in total disregard of those whom he must regard as the keepers of the national conscience, that is, the bishops and clergy of the Church of England.

The same sort of argument can be put in a different way. English 'folk religion' (a phenomenon recently given much prominence in Anglican circles, and worthy of much more attention by Free Church people) is, it is claimed, fundamentally Anglican. When English people without any personal commitment to Christian faith, but with a certain residual respect for Christian teaching which comes to the surface in times of personal or national crisis, wish to be married, or to bring their children to be baptized, or their relatives to be buried or cremated, they resort in nearly all cases, it is said, to the Church of England, and usually do so without considering any alternative. Moreover, on this argument, the 'public faith' (as Archbishop Habgood aptly calls it) of the English people – that is, their deeply buried but still real belief in God and certain values – is at root Anglican.

This being so, it is argued, the Church of England should remain established, in order to maintain and nourish, and, if possible, transform into a deeper Christian commitment, this latent faith, this 'anonymous Christianity' (as Karl Rahner calls it).

Moreover, it is said by Anglican Establishmentarians, the most notorious evils of Establishment, the Crown's appointment of bishops and Parliament's control of worship, have now been considerably modified, and are surely tolerable in their present form for the sake of a continued partnership between church and state. This is not an easy pill for Free Church people to swallow, but even that might be achieved by some of us on the understanding that further reforms of the system are to follow in the near future.[3]

But we also understand very clearly why many Anglicans wish the Establishment to come to an end. These Anglicans are not persuaded that the revised system of episcopal appointments meets the argument that the Church of Christ must be free under the gospel to choose its own pastors, since the Crown, however courteous and considerate its wearer may be, still has the last word. Even the reformed General Synod, in the last resort, is not autonomous, but acts under the ultimate authority of the Queen in Parliament. The Book of Common Prayer remains permanently available, not by the will of the church (which could conceivably in the future not will it), but by statute, and it cannot be altered or withdrawn without the approval of Parliament. The Alternative Service Book (1980) shows by its very title that it comprises 'alternatives' only – kindly permitted by Parliament.[4]

Some Anglicans indeed would put these arguments even more strongly.[5] The worst element in the situation is not that the Church of England lacks freedom in the vital areas of appointing pastors and ordering worship – bad though these things are – but that it acquiesces and sometimes even rejoices in its subordination to the State.[6]

These are the traditional objections to Establishment, re-stated and still cogent. We also appreciate the fairly new point made by Anglican reformers that Establishment places the Church of England in an entirely false position in the modern world, and especially from two points of view:

1. The Catholic Church of Jesus Christ, like God himself, has no favourites. It is committed to no political party, no nation-state, no section of the community; it has no interest in the *status quo* as such, or in violent or peaceful revolution as such. It is committed solely to the proclamation and furtherance of the kingdom of God, which covers the whole of human life, personal, social and political, and is open to all men and women and all human societies without any discrimination whatever. Its members from time to time will see it as their Christian duty to support nations, and normally their own nation, or parties or other groupings of people within their nation, which seem to them to be likely to promote Christian aims, although they may well differ as to which is the most suitable for the purpose; but their support will be conditional on the sincerity and continuance of such promotion. The church itself cannot align or identify itself with any particular human grouping whatever.

But an established church is necessarily connected with the interests of one particular nation, which may or may not, at any given time, be concerned to promote Christian principles.[7] The dangerous consequences of such a connexion are clear enough from the experiences of the Evangelical churches in Germany during the time of Hitler. The Church of England has not yet found itself in the predicament of the German Protestants at that time, though it could do so in the future. But this is not all. There is also a strong connexion, which is not strictly necessary, but has so far proved indissoluble, between the Church of England and one particular section of the English nation – with those who possess the major amount of power, wealth and security. And to calm the angry protest which may arise at these words, let it be said at once that ever since the time of the Christian Socialists and of the Anglo-Catholic priests who set up communities and worked self-sacrificially in the darkest slums of London and other cities, right up to the present time when the Bishop of Liverpool identifies himself with the cause of the poor, there have been very many people and groups of people, clerical and lay, within the Church of England, who have striven with all their might to loosen the connexion and to shake off the image which it creates of the Church of England as the friend of the 'haves'; and in their own personal cases they have certainly succeeded. Yet the image remains, and behind it a strong measure of reality. The Church of England, as a church, established by law and constituted as it is, is allied with those who have power, and not with the powerless; the presence of bishops in the House of Lords, the palaces or large houses in which, however modestly, they are bound to live, and the security in finance and prestige (now much diminished, of course) which the clergy enjoy, perpetuate the reality and give colour to the image.

2. The Church of Jesus Christ is both priestly and prophetic. It is charged with the task of mediating to its members the grace of the sacraments, which is unchangeably offered to all people. For its priestly purposes it preserves the regular ministry of word and sacraments through its liturgy and ordained ministry. This commission an established church is well-qualified to discharge, partly because of its close relations with those in political authority, and, in England and elsewhere, because of its tenure of the buildings, small and great, which are best for the exercise of a priestly role.

But the church's *prophetic* ministry includes the obligation to speak out, not only the faith as it has been delivered by tradition to our own time, but also the Word of God as it is particularly addressed to our generation; and this may – in fact, it almost certainly will – involve criticism of the existing order, of currently received ideas, and from time to time of the government of the day. To deny this, or to be mute when the Word of God has to be spoken by the church, is to repudiate the prophetic tradition of the Bible, Old Testament and New; it is to forego the freedom of the gospel.

Can an established church be truly prophetic? In particular, can the Church of England be truly prophetic? These are not rhetorical questions; they are invested with an urgent reality by the events of our time. The Falklands conflict is very much a case in point. Christian opinions may, and do, differ about the rightness of government policy before the conflict, and about the justification for the sending of the Task Force (though not about the skill and courage of the leaders and members of that Force). Probably on these matters, still disputed, the Church of England was no more unanimous in its understanding of the word of God than any other Christian body. But as to the character of the national service of worship at the end of the conflict there was a clear disparity between the intention of the government, which wished, quite simply, just to thank God for victory, and that of the Church of England, as represented by its leaders, which wished to thank God for the ending of war and to pray for speedy reconciliation. In the end the wishes of the church for the service it wanted to have in one of its own cathedrals prevailed, to the chagrin of several members of the government, who no doubt have taken due note of what happened. It is reliably reported – and if this report is true, it is highly significant for the future – that the Anglican authorities were largely enabled to insist on the kind of service which they wished for by the refusal of the Cardinal Archbishop of Westminster and the Moderator of the Free Church Council to take part in any other kind of service.

The report called *The Church and the Bomb*, prepared not by the Church of England as such but by a group of people asked by the Church of England to prepare it,[8] and not exclusively composed of Anglicans, created much disquiet in government circles, where the fear was born and began to grow that the Church of England was 'going over' to unilateralism. It was a fear not limited to those Members of Parliament who indulged in hysterical outbursts and appeared to regard the Church of England as a department of the Civil Service. Many quite serious politicians and church people scented danger. Their fears were no doubt allayed by the voting in the General Synod, but even after this those bishops who had spoken against the report were given special encouragement by government officials to explain and support government policy in public. And how can it ever be known whether voters in the Synod were to any extent swayed by the thought that for the

Synod to back the Report would set the church and the government at odds with each other? The church of Christ ought never to be in a position in which that question can even be asked. The whole incident brought some skeletons out of the cupboard, which have, of course, been rapidly replaced. But their existence can no longer be denied.

But what of the argument from folk religion? The facts of the matter are not quite as stated by ardent establishmentarians. The folk religion here described is real and widespread. But it is not universally Anglican in its flavour; the social and religious history, and the present situation, of England, as we shall see later in this chapter, are a great deal more complicated than that, and Anglican pervasiveness is somewhat limited. But even if the facts *were* exactly as they have just been set out, does the Church of England need to be established to deal with them in the most constructively pastoral way? In this connexion Peter Cornwell asks in *Church and Nation* what will really strengthen the open and gentle Anglican pastoral tradition:

> Assuredly not the establishment, with its counterfeit openness suggesting that, despite everything, England remains deep-down Christian, and Church of England at that; not that national Christianity which offers the gift of grace without calling for hard decision and commitment . . . Indeed, to lean upon the broken reed of the state connection with its redundant and distorting symbols prevents us from engaging in the real task of digging to that rock of the gospel, the holy catholicity of Christ himself.[9]

A Free Church person, especially, perhaps, if he is a Methodist, can – though not perhaps without a considerable effort – understand those Anglicans who say that the arguments for and against Establishment are nicely poised, and that while this is so there is no good ground for disturbing the existing order. But there is another argument which Anglicans do not always know about or find easy to appreciate, but which must here be put forward. It is an argument which must be set out with some care, if misunderstanding is to be avoided. It is concerned not with

Establishment in itself but with what goes with it in English life.

Before it can even be set out the reader is asked to be patient while certain facts about the English religious and social situation are indicated; not with scientific exactness, for that is impossible, but in general terms. Devoutly practising Anglicans probably outnumber the totality of devoutly practising members of other Christian churches in England if we leave out the Roman Catholic Church, but not if we include it. Nominal Anglicans outnumber the totality of nominal members of other churches to a much greater extent, since the religion of nominal Christians is usually stated by the people themselves to be Anglican when filling in forms, entering military service or asking the vicar to marry them. The Roman Catholic Church is the second largest of the 'mainstream' English churches; it is followed at some distance by the Methodist Church, the Baptist Churches, and the United Reformed Church, in that order (the Methodist Church is somewhat stronger in numbers than the Baptist and United Reformed Churches put together).

It is better to show these comparisons by general statements (even though they may be endlessly disputed) than by statistics, for the figures of membership given are calculated differently in different denominations.

'Nominal' Christians are not to be disregarded in the present connexion since they point to the amount of vague influence exerted by Christian churches on those who no longer make any practice of religious observance. But 'nominal Christianity' is plainly a very indeterminate factor in the whole religious situation.

The number of Anglican men and women of communicant status who have received higher education, and occupy positions of influence in the professions, the armed services, politics, commerce and industry, is disproportionately larger, in relation to total Anglican membership, than is to be found among non-Anglicans. Some would say that this is due to the 'old boy' nexus, and there are no doubt very many more Anglicans than non-Anglicans at public schools; but the real reasons are that Anglicans tend to come from the class in society which has the easiest access, at present, to the universities, and especially to Oxbridge, and that 'successful' Free Church people have often joined the Church of England for social reasons. The disproportion is steadily declining, and will continue to do so; but it is still significantly large. There are financial consequences of this; but more important are the greater sophistication and the greater attachment to culture in the aesthetic and intellectual sense, and to the social and sporting pursuits associated with the wealthier classes, that are to be found in Anglican than in Free Church or Roman Catholic circles. Among other things, the traditional association, now lapsing, of Free Church religion with the temperance movement sometimes puts Free Church people at a social disadvantage when they are enjoying Anglican hospitality.

These facts are fairly familiar, and readily explicable in terms of English religious and social history. There is another set of facts, also traceable to historical causes, which has not received the same amount of attention. The Church of England, as we have seen, is an authentically English institution. But there are other, no doubt smaller, Christian institutions which are just as authentically English as the Church of England – the Free Churches, and the Roman Catholic Church. All of these, as most Christians in England now recognize, share the basic teachings of the Church Catholic on God, man and salvation, with the Church of England.

But there are theological and liturgical differences, largely of emphasis, between them. Some differences arise from the unwillingness of one church or another to accept a particular tenet about the sacraments or the ministry as intrinsic to the faith. There are also some differences in life-style and ethical approach. These various differences express themselves in the institutional life of the various denominations.

Yet there is no justification at all for denying the title 'English' to any of these denominations, some of them nearly as old as the Church of England itself as it was ordered separately from Rome; and the Roman Catholic Church is in a sense older still. They are, in fact, as English as the Church of England itself.

The Independents, or Congregationalists, now joined with the English Presbyterians to form the United Reformed Church, lay much stress on the 'Crown Rights of the Redeemer', over against the claims of a clerical hierarchy, and on the presence of Christ within the individual congregation in which the Church Catholic is focussed and every believer has equal status. Who can say that this is anything but authentically English Christianity, with its Englishness validated by the very fact that the 'democracy' of the Church Meeting was one of the organic antecedents of English political democracy? Many English Presbyterians are, it is true, of Scottish origin, but within the United Reformed Church they represent the sturdily maintained right of English people to stand up, if necessary, to secular authority in the name of conscience and the word of God. The Baptists underline the supreme importance of personal conversion to Jesus Christ in their practice of Believers' Baptism, as against automatic or mechanical incorporation in the Body of Christ by rites and ceremonies alone; it is not difficult to recognize there the English persistence in individual faith and individual decision. If the Baptists are not authentically English in their Christianity, how is it that the Baptist book *Pilgrim's Progress* is so beloved by English Christians of every school of thought?

These three groups can be said, in fairness to all of them, to be derived in part from the Puritanism which entered England from Geneva and Scotland, was speedily assimilated and naturalized by the English, and has penetrated every non-Roman Church in this country. The evangelical section of the Church of England is Puritan through and through. This is sometimes denied recognition, or regarded as a serious defect, but chiefly because 'Puritanism' is usually employed in a narrow, pejorative sense, and the true character of our Puritan forefathers has been forgotten.

The Methodists, arriving later on the scene, have always tried to have the best of both worlds – by combining orderly worship on the Anglican model with the spontaneity and flexibility needed for evangelism and favoured by the Nonconformist churches, by uniting personal salvation with the corporate experience of the Catholic Church in the fellowship of the Holy Spirit, and by creating an active partnership between the ordained ministry and the laity. They have not always succeeded in this praiseworthy attempt, but the effort is as valid an expression of English spirituality as the Anglican combination of 'Catholics' and 'Protestants' in one church.

The Roman Catholics are a special case. Until a generation ago it was not wholly illegitimate to regard them as forming a ghetto-like community consisting of Irish immigrants in large numbers and a small but select body of aristocratic 'recusant' families which had survived constant hardship until Catholic Emancipation in 1829. This is now no longer true. The 'Irish immigrants' are largely integrated into the English nation, and while the Catholic families are still important, Roman Catholicism has shown itself able to commend itself to English people who prefer an authoritarian, somewhat clerical religion, so long as it leads to worship which engages all the senses as well as the mind, and is genuinely aware of actual human needs.

These non-Anglican churches have all contributed in effective and far-reaching ways to the political and social life of England as well as its religious life. The Independents, Presbyterians and Baptists did this in the seventeenth century and after; the Roman Catholics recently, once they were able to emerge from the catacombish existence imposed on them by post-Reformation English society; and the Methodists most widely and deeply, by early Trade Unionism and the non-Marxist wing of the Labour Movement, and in the nineteenth century by the aspirations of the bourgeoisie. It is not an exaggeration to say that Nonconformity, Methodism and Roman Catholicism – bedfellows not so uncongenial as one might be tempted to think – have strangely and almost unconsciously combined to form a pervasive element in English politics, national and civic, which in its Liberal, Labour and now Social Democratic forms, has acted as a powerful counterpoise to Anglican-conservative defence of the established order, and so helped in the peaceful, point and counterpoint development of English democracy. Nowadays it finds its organ of expression in *The Guardian*, the mouthpiece of educated Nonconformity, even though that newspaper does not always recognize its Christian affiliations.

All the non-Anglican communities have lived, and prospered or declined, under the shadow of the Church of England as the established church. Until recently they had to formulate their teaching and order their lives under conditions, first of all of persecution, then of harassment, and then of social disadvantage. This experience has, on the one hand, often, but not always, made them defensive and aggressive by turns, apologetic, resentful and competitive – in other words given them a minority-consciousness. On the other hand it has strengthened their self-reliance and devotion to their own distinctiveness. In recent years, with the easement of restrictions and the increasing hospitality and friendliness of the Church of England, they have been able to live more freely and naturally, and more in accordance with their own understanding of the gospel; and their ministers and people have been able to learn from the Church of England without incurring the taunt of treachery or sycophancy within their own ranks. The Church of England has also been prepared, as it was not in the past, to learn from them. This is undeniably a fruitful development and can be more fruitful still.

The upshot of all this can be expressed geographically, although accuracy is once again impossible. Throughout most of rural England, and in nearly all the towns and cities of the East, the South East and the South, and of the West so far as the Tamar, the Church of England occupies a dominant position, as measured by church attendance and influence on non-religious life. In Cornwall (rural and urban), the Black Country, some of the Yorkshire dales, the Durham coalfield and certain other areas of the industrial North, Methodism occupies a position which approximates to dominance so far as the general religious ethos is concerned. The same is true of Roman Catholicism in parts of Liverpool and in some other Lancashire towns. In Bristol Anglicans and non-Anglicans enjoy a kind of parity;[10] the same has been true from time to time in Birmingham, Manchester and Sheffield. In the other great cities, at least so far as their suburbs are concerned, the Free Churches, taken together, amount to somewhat less in strength than the Church of England; in central London there are not many signs of Free Church activity, in the London suburbs the situation is much the same as in the suburbs of other large cities. All in all the state of affairs revealed by the 1851 census, when it was shown that nearly half the churchgoing population attended non-Anglican churches, has since then varied moderately in the direction of Anglican preponderance.[11]

It is against the background of these facts that we can go on to state and consider the additional argument which a non-Anglican is bound to bring to the Establishment debate, and to bring it without rancour – an argument, to repeat, not from the institution of Establishment itself, but from a significant accompaniment of that institution. It is the argument from the 'Establishment attitude', an attitude still pervasive in this country, an attitude not limited to churchpeople, though most frequently found among them, but also reflected in large sections of the media and large parts of the general public.

But before this attitude is described it is necessary for me to pause for a moment more and to say, wholeheartedly and explicitly, that it is not shared by the large group of Anglicans who are committed to ecumenism, and is in fact deeply deplored by them; together with Free Church people and Roman Catholics – all of whom have had their 'attitudes' in the past – these Anglicans have reached a relationship of mutual friendship and respect which rules out the 'Establishment attitude' as inappropriate and indefensible.

The attitude is that of regarding non-Anglicans, consciously or unconsciously, as inferior Christians. In a book published in 1962 (*Methodists and Unity*) I wrote that Anglicans frequently evince the 'consciousness of effortless superiority' which was once ascribed to the members of a famous Oxford college (as my own college was in question, I could say this with lessened embarrassment). I do not think that this is as true as it was twenty years ago, or true of so many Anglicans; but it is still, painfully, true.[12]

The attitude is at root paternalistic (or maternalistic), of the same nature as the ingrained feelings of many English people towards the members of their former colonial empire, and of many men towards women; it is for the most part, in these days, benevolent, but nonetheless humiliating for that; it is directed towards non-Anglicans not as individuals, but towards them as members of second-class religious communities (sometimes called 'sects'), whose spiritual or intellectual achievements, when they are noticed at all, are greeted with kindly surprise. The attitude, of course, embodies itself in certain concrete situations, as when it is taken for granted that the vicar or rector will take the chair and the initiative on all ecumenical occasions, resting on his prerogative as rector or vicar of the parish, and that if he disapproves, the action proposed will not be carried out; that what a bishop says or does has inevitable priority over what even the most learned, or even the holiest and wisest, non-Anglican may say or do; that the Church of Jesus Christ, after gracious reference has been made to the presence of non-Anglicans on the ecumenical scene, is in the last resort identical and coterminous with the Church of England, and may be referred to accordingly; that the Church of England knows what is best for the other churches, and that in any case that they will one day, if they are wise, come back to Mother. It is the attitude crystallized in Voltaire's description of the Church of England as 'l'Eglise par excellence'.[13]

Two typical examples of something which all readers will easily recognize from their own experience, both coming from highly reputable quarters, will suffice to illustrate the point at issue.

J. R. H. Moorman's *History of the Church in England* (1952) (*in* England, be it noted, not *of* England), a work of much scholarship, widely used in theological training, refers to the Congregationalists and Baptists (as 'sectaries'), at the time of their first emergence in England, and then never again in the rest of his book (except that the participation of Congregationalists in the Church of South India is once mentioned). Dr (later Bishop) Moorman's writing was presumably governed by certain principles of Christian historiography, and it is fairly clear what some of them were.

The second example shows the Establishment attitude in its unconscious form. A diocese which has a good claim to be the most ecumenical of all dioceses recently invited nine 'Partners in Mission' (five Anglicans and four non-Anglicans, oddly enough) from several nations, to come into its parishes for a few weeks to discover 'the needs for the mission of the church' and the ways in which they can be met. Its report starts, very properly, with a theological description of 'the church' (presumably the Holy

Catholic Church, but perhaps the Church of England) as 'essentially missionary'; and then for the rest of its course simply assumes the complete identity of 'the church' with the Church of England, without any mention of the other churches. Yet these churches quite certainly, as every Christian in the diocese knows, or should know, are engaged in active living partnership, and in partnership in *mission*, with the Church of England throughout the diocese, and most notably in Local Ecumenical Projects (more numerous than in any other diocese). This fact means, surely, that the parishes in question cannot usefully be looked at simply as they are in themselves, as if they were self-sufficient and independent communities, but must be seen always in many particulars as they are in relation to their neighbour churches, their active partners and co-worshippers. No one would claim to give a full account of the member of a family by looking at him or her alone; our relationships and partnerships are part of what we are. Yet the reporting team in this case scarcely even noticed that these parishes' 'partnership in mission' extended beyond the confines of the parish church. Perhaps one reason for this distressing failure was the acknowledged omission to consult any Free Church leaders or people throughout the team's visit to the diocese. But of course the malaise goes deeper than this.

Some justifications of the attitude have been put forward. One is theological: according to certain doctrines of Apostolic Succession, Anglican priests have a higher status before God than their Free Church counterparts. But these doctrines, however sincerely held, scarcely justify superciliousness towards those who hold a different doctrine and practise a different tradition. Nor are they doctrines which are accepted by all Anglicans or go very far back into Anglican history. Sometimes, in fact, as they are stated they sound very much like rationalizations of a preconceived social assumption. And the attitude in question is often exhibited towards Roman Catholic priests, who do not labour under the theological disadvantage of Free Church ministers, but are like them members of a non-Anglican community.

Another possible justification is grounded in the parish system, itself an aspect of the Establishment. 'I am the priest of this parish;

therefore other priests and ministers are here by intrusion or by my permission', is the thought in many clerical minds, and it is historically understandable. But since by common consent the parish system, except in a decreasing number of rural areas, no longer corresponds to the actual Christian situation, and since in the towns and cities it is physically impossible for the Anglican incumbent to care for all the people who live in his parish, this justification, which could never excuse superciliousness, nowadays lacks any real force of any kind; it is a relic from the past.

But if we can find no Christian justification for the Establishment attitude, it is not hard to trace the cause of it. It is, quite simply, the Establishment itself. The conflicts and legislation of the sixteenth and seventeenth centuries created religious and social divisions in English society which have become set in concrete. The Establishment has injected into the blood of most Anglicans – not all, of course – an element which must be called pride of position and of orthodoxy. The disabilities of non-Anglicans have been largely removed, but the infection of the blood remains. Nowadays this infection is much more social than religious. It is persistent, insidious and gently corrosive of church relationships. It constitutes the most serious single obstacle to the unity of the church, and therefore to its whole mission; indeed it contradicts the very nature of the church. It will continue as long as the Establishment survives. Does it not constitute, in and by itself, a convincing argument for disestablishment, or at least for a radical revision of the present state of affairs?

Note on Royal Marriages and the Act of Settlement

The Act of Settlement, 1701, enacted after a period of bitter disputes between Catholics and Protestants in this country and elsewhere, and while the memories of these disputes still rankled in the minds of all classes, stipulates precisely that no one may inherit the throne who 'is or shall be reconciled to or shall hold communion with the see or Church of Rome, or shall profess the popish religion or shall marry a papist'. In recent times the veto on the Sovereign's marriage to a papist has become a matter for serious discussion. It is widely thought that the Sovereign and his or her heir should be entitled to marry the person of his or her own choice, and that the slur on Roman Catholics, cast by the clause in the Act, should be removed.

The present Government does not intend to take any action in this matter. The General Synod of the Church of England debated it in November 1982, but did not proceed to a vote.

Those who support a change in the law argue for the most part that the question of the Establishment, which they have no wish to destroy, is not involved. But it is surely hard to accept this. If the Sovereign marries a Roman Catholic, the Roman Catholic partner is obliged by loyalty to his or her own church 'to do all in his power to have all the children baptized and brought up in the [Roman] Catholic Church'. 'All the children' include the heir to the throne. If the heir to the throne grows up as a Roman Catholic, the result, under the present legislation, will be that he or she will have to abjure either his faith or the succession. Is this in any way satisfactory? But it is a result closely bound up with the Establishment, under the force of which it is clearly necessary for the Supreme Governor of the Church of England to be a member of that church.[14]

(Oddly enough, the heir to the throne, or the Sovereign, may freely marry a Free Church person.)

5

Ecumenical Contradictions

Anyone who relied on the British media for news of the Sixth Assembly of the World Council of Churches in Vancouver, in the summer of 1983, could be excused for thinking that the Church of England played a prominent part in the proceedings. For it was only the utterances and actions of English Anglican ecclesiastics, for the most part, which received favourable coverage.

Individual Anglicans did, indeed, make an impression on the Assembly, which represented three hundred churches on a world scale. But the Church of England as such, though it occupied a high place at one time, seems to many observers to have slipped a long way down the ecumenical league-table in recent years. It may be regarded as still in the first division, it is said, but only just.

Is this a true judgment? The question is complicated and deserves careful scrutiny. In 1910, after some initial reluctance on the part of the Archbishop of Canterbury (Randall Davidson), the Church of England, followed by the other churches of the Anglican communion, threw its weight behind the Edinburgh Missionary Conference at Edinburgh, usually regarded as the effective start of the Ecumenical Movement. The Edinburgh Conference led to a great variety of ecumenical activity on a wide scale, notably the Faith and Order and Life and Work Movements, whose work was interrupted, but not stopped, by the First World War; and always to the fore in the many great and small conferences that were held, in Lausanne, Stockholm, Edinburgh (again), Oxford and elsewhere during the inter-war years were Archbishop William Temple, Bishop G. K. A. Bell, and the Anglican layman, J. H. Oldham; and these men seemed to be carrying the Church of England, or great sections of it, with them.

Above all, the 'Appeal' of the Bishops of the Anglican communion, meeting in Lambeth in 1920, 'to all Christian People', to engage in discussions with a view to unity on the basis of the Lambeth Quadrilateral, gave a powerful fillip to ecumenical hopes and expectations throughout the world, and not least in England. 'Here is the Church of England giving the lead to which its historic role and dignity entitle it'; this was the thought in the minds of ecumenists everywhere. The response to the Appeal was widespread and sincere. The difficulties soon appeared; but until the Second War the persistent quest for unity in England went on, still under the leadership of the Church of England.

Then at the end of that war came the invitation of Archbishop Geoffrey Fisher to the English Free Churches to establish communion with the Church of England by 'taking episcopacy into their systems'. The Church of England promoted the conference with the Free Churches which worked out the implications of such an action, and asked any church which wished to do so to take the matter further in conversations designed to lead to a practical issue. The Church of Scotland and the Presbyterian Church of England were the first to respond, by activating conversations already started, but these conversations virtually ceased when the General Assembly of the Church of Scotland in 1959 rejected the proposals which emerged.

So far the Church of England had showed itself eager to enter into communion with the other churches in the country; yet perhaps reservations were beginning to appear in certain minds – reservations which prevented it, and have continued to prevent it, from entering into full communion with the Church of South India which Anglican representatives had done so much to promote, formulate and bring into existence.[1] In 1958 the Methodist Church, accepting the Anglican invitation, began official conversations with the Church of England; in 1965 the method proposed by the Commission, and approved by all its Anglican members, of uniting the churches in two stages was overwhelmingly supported by the governing bodies of both churches. But in 1969 the scheme worked out on the basis of what had been already agreed, and approved by the Methodist Conference, failed to receive a large enough majority in the Anglican Convocations; and when the objections brought by its opponents had been largely dealt with by a slight revision of the proposals, the newly constituted General Synod of the church gave it a somewhat smaller majority than that of 1969. So the Scheme fell through.

This result was greatly to the displeasure of a large number of Anglicans, and it was they, rather than the Methodists, who freely employed the simile of the bride jilted at the altar. These Anglicans, who on any reasonable reckoning, formed a clear majority of the membership and clergy of their church, made heroic efforts during the seventies to repair the harm that had been done in terms of church relations and the mission of the church to this country. They promoted conferences from which the idea of a 'covenant for visible unity', in which the recently formed United Reformed Church,[2] the Churches of Christ and the Moravian Church, in addition to the Methodists, were ready to join, was developed; they gave wholehearted support to the Covenanting Proposals which ultimately appeared. But when the matter came before the General Synod the necessary majority, though a smaller one was required than on the previous occasion, was not forthcoming; indeed, there was a smaller vote for the Covenant than for the Anglican-Methodist Scheme of 1969.

At about the same time as the Church of England rejected the Anglican-Methodist Scheme, it accepted the Scheme for the formation of the Church of North India which was consummated in 1970. This was a puzzling, though welcome, fact to many people, since the principles which underlay the unification of the ministries in North India were the same as those which underlay the rejected Service of Reconciliation in the Anglican-Methodist Scheme. Distance seems to have lent a particular sort of enchantment to the view.

The Church of England was enthusiastic in helping to launch

the British Council of Churches in 1946, and has provided an archiepiscopal President ever since. In the early days Anglican leaders were notably enterprising in the affairs of the Council. But the Church of England has never given the financial help to the Council which its resources would suggest that it is capable of giving; and for some time now it has not given the impression of being firmly behind the Council, preferring to send as its representatives sober and carefully chosen, but not necessarily very ecumenical, spokesmen of the various parties within the church. The debates in the Assembly of the Council, as a result, have not always been exciting, and the actions to which the Council has wished to commit itself have lacked the real and substantial backing of the Church of England.

In the World Council of Churches Anglican bishops and theologians have always been recognized as wise statesmen from a church rich in valuable traditions. This was especially true of Archbishop Michael Ramsey. In Faith and Order matters, Patrick Rodger and Oliver Tomkins, both later to become bishops, and others in the tradition of William Temple and George Bell, have been greatly trusted and very influential. But, somehow, from the time of the Uppsala Assembly of 1968 until now, and in spite of the importance of individual leaders of thought, the Church of England has lost sympathetic interest in the WCC, and the WCC has not taken the Church of England as seriously as once it did. This is, of course, partly due to the fact that in the WCC the churches of the West, and of the First World, have yielded many of their places in the centre of the stage to the growing, and growingly articulate, churches of the Third World – which is, indeed, as it should be. The Church of England has responded to the express wish of the WCC. But this is not the sole cause.

A striking feature of the situation is that the English bishops on the whole have maintained a high standard of ecumenical leadership, and have voted for moves towards unity and for schemes of union and covenant by large majorities. It is a body of parochial clergy (parochial in mind, perhaps, as well as in location) and especially of those who believe most strongly that the Anglican episcopacy is of divine origin, which, with many professions of devotion to unity, have refused to take the practical steps which unity requires, and have succeeded in preventing their church from doing so either. They have also helped to cool the enthusiasm of their church for international ecumenism.

The upshot of all this is that the Church of England, more than sixty years after the Lambeth Appeal, is in full communion with no other churches in Christendom except those of the Anglican Communion, the Old Catholics, the Churches of Sweden and Finland and the Church of North India – amounting to a rather small proportion of the three hundred churches in the World Council of Churches.[3]

This is a tale which no Christian can recount with pleasure. Yet it shows that the allegation of ecumenical decline is not un-supported by the facts. There is, of course, another side to the matter, the rapprochement with Rome, to which we shall turn. And there are signs of a new involvement among younger men and women theologians and activists. The Archbishop of York has now become a member of the Central Committee of the WCC, and Bishop Austin Baker of its Faith and Order Commission. But there has been a long gap.

In the case of a church committed by its theology and its Canon Law, and by its own statesmanship during the present century, to the pursuit of unity, this sad tendency calls for an explanation.

Theological considerations are plainly important. There are many Anglicans, including some theologians of repute, who hold that 'the Holy Catholic Church consists of the Roman Catholic Church, the Orthodox Churches and the Churches of the Anglican Communion' (in the words, or virtually the words, that were posted in a number of parish churches one or two decades ago). They believe that no one can legitimately preside at the eucharist who is not ordained to the priesthood within one or other of the churches which constitute the Holy Catholic Church. The ministries and sacraments of all other churches (or so-called churches) are alike invalid, though the ministers may be worthy people and their sacramental services edifying. On this view, if there is to be full communion, let alone organic union, between

78

the Church of England and other bodies (to use a word that was once often used in this connexion), or 'ecclesial communities' (to use the language of Vatican II), their ministers must be unmistakeably incorporated within the historic ministry of the Church of England, or some other constituent part of the Holy Catholic Church; and it goes without saying that all subsequent ordinations within these 'bodies' must be carried out by bishops in the historic succession.

This view is unambiguously clear, and has a respectable and reputable history within the Church of England, though the passionate and uncritical intensity with which it is held by some of its proponents may be partly due to the Anglican practice, now diminished, of maintaining theological colleges in which only one doctrine of the church and ministry is taught. But this doctrine is not one of the authoritative doctrines of the Church of England; it has not been uninterruptedly taught in that church, and it is held by only a minority of theologically responsible Anglicans today.

Those who hold it are usually to be found opposing the ordination of women. The theological arguments on this matter are discussed elsewhere in this book,[4] and they are not necessarily bound up with the theological viewpoint just outlined, except to the extent that the non-Anglican churches which hold a similar view of the ministry do not ordain women either, but in practice this 'high' view of the ministry and opposition to women priests seem to go together in the same people. (At least, this has been true up to now, though the situation may be changing).

It is easy to see why those who are of this mind are lukewarm towards the World Council of Churches and the British Council of Churches; and take sometimes a lordly attitude, and sometimes a regretful but negative attitude, towards local co-operation. It is even easier to see why they voted solidly against the Anglican-Methodist Scheme and the Covenanting Proposals, on the understandable ground that these projects did not include the unmistakeable incorporation of Free Church ministries into the historic succession, and, in the case of the Covenanting Proposals, included women as well as men ministers. Every possible effort was made by the negotiators to make provision for their point of view and their practice, which no one wished to exclude from the comprehensiveness of the Church of England, or from the later, hoped-for, united church. But since their own point of view and their practice are by their very nature exclusive, even sectarian, it is not at all surprising that these efforts failed.

In the case of the Anglican-Methodist Scheme, but not to any marked extent in the case of the Covenanting Proposals, another minority, the one made up of the Conservative Evangelicals, was in the picture. They opposed the Scheme on theological grounds almost exactly opposite to those of the Anglo-Catholics: they held that Free Church ministers were already ordained as ministers of word and sacraments in the Church of God. Taking their stand on scripture, they scouted the notion of historic succession, and seemed (to the outsider at least) to have much less use for bishops than had the non-episcopal churches. Therefore they spoke and voted against a Scheme which required Methodist ministers to 'go through' a Service of Reconciliation which could be interpreted (though it was not, of course, so interpreted by the Methodist Church) as an ordination. It is likely that some of them were also apprehensive that union with the Methodists would in due course upset the existing relationship between their church and the state, endanger the position of evangelicals within the church, and question the authoritativeness of the Thirty-Nine Articles – those features of the Church of England which they believed to be grounded in scripture.

Once again, it is easy to see why their beliefs obliged them to vote against the Anglican-Methodist Scheme, and some of them to vote against the Covenanting Proposals, though here also every effort to persuade them not to do so was made both by Methodists (who are their fellow-evangelicals) and by those Anglicans who held a more moderately 'evangelical' position. The Conservative Evangelicals are as firmly exclusive of other views of the church and ministry than their own as are the Anglo-Catholics. Nor can they perhaps be expected, on the basis of a theology of salvation which regards all others as unsound, to co-operate warmly with other churches in their locality, or with the British or World Council of Churches, of whose doctrinal basis they gravely disapprove. It is very gratifying therefore that evangelicals of all nations present at the Vancouver Assembly published an Open Letter afterwards in which they said that, having actually experienced and participated in the workings and worship of the World Council, they now realized the great contribution to the mission and unity of the church the Council was making. It will take some time for English Evangelicals not at the Assembly to weigh this statement, and perhaps to change an attitude which has been very evident up to the present time, and has certainly not helped the ecumenical enterprise.

Now Anglo-Catholics and Conservative Evangelicals form two minorities in the Church of England. They are both very articulate; they can call on some not inconsiderable resources of scholarship; in each group there are men and women of deep spirituality. But neither of them speaks for the Church of England. If they are added together they still constitute a minority, and still less in that case can they speak for the church since they contradict one another on many, to them, essential points.

So why does their negative attitude to ecumenism, theologically based though it may be, prevail against the convictions of the generality of churchpeople, of teachers, theologians and parish clergy, and of the great majority of the bishops? One straightforward reason given is that approval of the Anglican–Methodist Scheme or of the Covenanting Proposals would have 'split the church'. This is equivalent to saying that the unity of one particular church, the Church of England, is more important than the unity of the Body of Christ in the whole world. This is a narrow and 'self-preserving' view. In any case it was only the outward unity of the Church of England that was preserved in this way, for inwardly the Church of England was more divided by a negative vote than it would have been by a positive one. Nevertheless, this factor cannot be discounted; but it cannot offer a total explanation.

Perhaps much of this lies in the constitution of the Synod. It is a simple fact that in the case of the Anglican–Methodist Scheme, and to some extent in the case of the Covenanting Proposals, the two minorities by joining forces – which they had no scruple about doing, in spite of their deep differences from each other – produced a minority which was large enough among the clergy to prevent positive action from being taken. It is not necessary to know the exact opinions of those who voted negatively for the validity of this reason to be accepted.

Yet no rule of the constitutions, either of the Convocations in 1969, or of the General Synod subsequently, was broken. The whole disastrous operation was perfectly legal. In the light of this fact it was even possible for some to argue that the will of God had been manifested by the Convocations' and Synod's decision, on the assumption that the constitution of the Church of England, but not those of the Free Churches, was divinely (though mysteriously) originated. If that assumption is not accepted – and it seems dubious – it has to be admitted that a great deal of responsibility for two ecumenical failures must be placed on the constitution. That constitution does not perform the difficult task of eliciting and expressing the mind of the Church, the *sensus fidelium*.

But the question arises: why, so late as the 1960s in the case of the General Synod, was a constitution framed and approved which was likely to postpone indefinitely, and in some cases prevent absolutely, any substantial change of policy urged upon it by any party of reform, and in particular any union with another church in this country? It cannot surely be maintained that the framers of this constitution were so ignorant or innocent that they were not aware of the likelihood just pointed out. Or, if by any chance they *were* taken by surprise when certain things happened, why is there no disposition, except among the few, to change the provisions which have had this effect?

In other words, to blame the ecumenical failures of the Church of England largely on its constitution does not meet the case. We have to look below the constitution to the spirit and atmosphere in the Church of England which produced it and sustains it. And here we find at once, widespread among clergy and people, a profound unwillingness to change the *status quo* in any matter which affects the ordering of church life as it has come down from the past. It is an unwillingness which sometimes escalates into fear and panic; it does not seem ever to diminish or go away.

It will be objected at once that in the Church of England, as in other churches, there are always rebels, reformers and innovators. Indeed there are, and often they are of the highest quality, schooled in the spiritual and intellectual disciplines of Anglican saints and scholars, and aware to an acute extent of the special problems of the age in which we live. They are not silenced – to the credit of a church which has learned a painful lesson from its handling of John Wesley and John Henry Newman. But equally they do not get their way; they are listened to with great respect, and then the vote goes the other way. No one who was present will ever forget the speech made by Archbishop Michael Ramsey in the second debate on the Anglican-Methodist Scheme, in 1972, the reverent silence in which it was heard, the enthusiasm with which it was applauded – and the pre-determined vote with which it was rejected.

Resistance to change is common in all Christian denominations – indeed, perhaps, in all religious organizations. The ground of it is partly good: what has proved valuable to millions for centuries must not be lightly thrown away. So all forms of Christian faith are rightly, in this sense, conservative. But other, less worthy grounds can in a church masquerade as good ones, especially among clergy: a desire to retain a certain position and certain privileges in society, unwillingness to have one's decisions questioned or discussed by laypeople, a tendency to question the good faith of those who propose new ways of worship or thought, a sheer refusal to think out again questions 'settled' in one's youth. Who can say that these did not operate in the matter under discussion? Ecumenism in England certainly involved various threats to the *status quo*, and indeed to the status of Anglican clergy.

Christopher Lewis has drawn attention to the distinction, first made by American sociologists, between 'locals' and 'cosmopolitans', and applied it to the ecumenical scene.[5] 'Locals' are those who stay in the same place, often geographically, but certainly intellectually, all their lives; they are preoccupied with local concerns, to which they often devote themselves with sacrificial zeal.

'Cosmopolitans' are those who range over the world – geographically if they have the chance, and intellectually in any case; they are less concerned with local than universal questions. 'Locals' tend to be less ecumenical than 'cosmopolitans', or to be ecumenical on a narrower basis. Perhaps the Church of England has bred a greater proportion of 'locals' among its clergy than other churches, and perhaps the parochial and diocesan systems have contributed to this?

Two further strong reasons operate against ecumenism, one in respect of schemes of union with the Free Churches, the other on the international scale. Occasionally in the debates before the decisions on the Anglican–Methodist Scheme, frequently in the debates before the decisions on the Covenanting Proposals, opponents and objectors urged the Church of England to decline projects leading towards visible unity with the non-episcopal churches on the ground that such unity would delay, or probably prevent, the recognition of Anglican Orders by the Roman Catholic Church, and thus any form of union with Rome. This argument was of course reinforced by the presence in the Covenanting Proposals of the non-negotiable clause that women Free Church ministers should be recognized on exactly the same terms as men.

This was not a wholly reasonable objection. No recognized Roman Catholic authority had in either instance urged a negative response on the Church of England, though individual Roman Catholics may have done so (but individual and very responsible Roman Catholics had also urged a positive response). The time when Anglican Orders would be recognized was not likely to be in the near future (though the setting up of ARCIC[6] may have led some people to expect it soon); when it arrived, probably all Free Church ministers would be episcopally ordained, and so their orders would no longer be in question. The ordination of women was likely to be accepted by the Church of England in any case by then; it would not be visible unity with the Free Churches which caused *that* difficulty. Nor was it a *wise* objection; to hold off from closer relations with churches which the Church of England was already sharing in an intimate partnership of mission and worship in at least a thousand localities, and at the highest level of understanding among leaders and theologians, for the sake of a union which might never become a real possibility, is not part of a statesmanship which includes the unity of *all* Christian people in its purview, and it makes nonsense of the Anglican claim to be a bridge church. But whether reasonable or wise, or not, the objection certainly worked with many people, and was exploited, sometimes unscrupulously, by the opponents of unity with the Free Churches when dealing with their own constituencies.

The other reason is this. From the time of the Uppsala Assembly in 1968 the World Council of Churches, as we have seen, was more and more influenced by the church leaders of the Third World, and less and less by those of the West. Naturally, therefore, the issues of world-wide poverty, racial discrimination, neo-colonialism and economic and political domination, to which the Western churches had previously given very selective attention, came more and more into the centre of the picture. Anglicans, like other Western Christians, found themselves to be representa-tive targets for those who attacked oppression in the name of Christ and pleaded for a juster society. The 'Programme to Com-bat Racism', which invited financial contributions to a special fund (quite separate from the general funds of the WCC) designed to assist the social and educational development of oppressed and deprived racial groups, was caricatured in certain parts of the press, and in letters to the *Church Times*, as an incitement to terrorists, and this caricature was uncritically accepted as fact in many Eng-lish quarters. All this seems to have spread the notion through many parts of the Church of England that the WCC is an organization conspiring to subvert settled governments in various parts of the world; and Anglicanism in general, because of its history, and its position in English society, reacts strongly against any kind of subversion. The representatives of established order, it was felt, must stand shoulder to shoulder!

But having drawn attention to all these reasons, operating vari-ously in different parts of the Church of England, the analysis must be completed by the recognition of a factor, deep in the Anglican consciousness, which persistently permeates all its relations with non-Anglican Christians, English and foreign, unless it is identified and exorcised. This identification and exorcism have indeed taken place on a growing number of Anglicans at every level, and the process is going on. But they have not yet reached enough people and enough sections of Anglican institutional life to make the Church of England really ready for a thoroughgoing ecumenism.

The factor is this. The Church of England has enjoyed an unquestioned, and still unquestionable, intellectual and social pre-eminence over other Christians in this country for several centuries – in much the same way as Oxford and Cambridge until recently enjoyed pre-eminence in academic circles. This makes it very difficult for Anglicans, and Anglican teachers in particular, to see that they have anything to learn from Christians of other nations and other churches. Once they had not – or at least, not much. Now they have, at least a fair amount. There is no true ecumenical progress until each *church* – not just each individual, or most individuals, but each *church* – is ready to learn from each other church on terms of parity. The Anglican unwillingness to learn, nowadays usually unconscious, is a notable example of the 'Establishment attitude' which has already been discussed in another connexion.

Many Anglicans hope that the way to reunion with Rome will not be barred by the inhibitions and complexes which have bedevilled the attempts to bring closely together the Church of England and the Free Churches. At this particular stage of the new and exciting ecumenical development represented by the ARCIC reports, they seem to have good ground for this hope at least on the theological level, though it has to be remembered that in other such situations hopes have risen high only to be dashed, sometimes at the last moment. The progress made by ARCIC in the fulfilment of its mandate 'to discover each other's faith as it is today, and to appeal to history only for enlightenment, not as a way of perpetuating past controversy',[7] has been remarkable. This positive and constructive way of working together on which the Commission was thus launched has enabled it to eliminate the past misunderstandings and suspicions, and the many painful memories, which threatened to abort the whole enterprise at the start; and to produce statements of real agreement on issues which have caused bloodshed and continuing controversy for four hundred years.

The conception of the church as *koinonia*, which is that communion with God in Christ, and that sharing in the Holy Spirit, by which all the baptized are brought into communion with each other,[8] gives an underlying theme to the three statements brought together in the Final Report, and frees them from the institutional and jurisdictional emphasis which has often characterized 'catholic' pronouncements in the past. It sets the Commission free to explore the inner meaning of sacramental fellowship and ministerial authority. And if it slides, insensibly and no doubt unintentionally, into identifying the church, as *koinonia*, with the Roman Catholic Church plus the Anglican communion, the way is at least open for a more fully catholic understanding of the church in the future.

The treatment of the 'sacrifice of the Mass', by using the category of *anamnesis*,[9] allays the anxiety of those who think that Roman Catholic priests still claim to repeat the once-for-all sacrifice of Christ on the Cross; and at the same time reassures those who fear that the sacrificial element is in process of being drained out of Anglican liturgy. The early history of the Christian ministry is suitably released from the outdated notion that the threefold pattern is prescribed by the New Testament.[10] The relation of the priesthood of Christ to the priesthood of the laity and the priesthood of the ordained ministry is skilfully handled, without any trace of sacerdotalism,[11] and the place of *episcope* in the church is vindicated as the necessary implicate of *koinonia*.[12]

These are substantial achievements. There is a certain ambiguity at the crucial point where the presence of Christ in the eucharist is described and the philosophy of transubstantiation is discarded;[13] and again when the difference between the ministry of the priesthood and that of the laity is pointed out.[14] In the Statements on Authority there is a certain tendency to assume that what actually happened in history, for instance to the See of Rome, is necessarily what was divinely intended to happen, on the general ground that the Holy Spirit does not desert the church (in spite of the fact that it is acknowledged in the Report that in specific cases the church has disobeyed or misinterpreted the leading of the Spirit).[15] But these weaknesses, which can be corrected as the ARCIC process passes into another phase, do not invalidate the claim made by the Commission that 'the convergence reflected in our Final Report, would appear to call for the establishing of a new relationship between our churches as a next stage in the journey towards Christian unity'.[16]

But it would be dishonest not to point out that the optimism engendered by the Final Report has to be tempered by the realization that certain awkward facts about the Church of England remain to be faced. And it has to be added that a certain danger looms up in the minds of non-Anglican friends of the Church of England.

There is a strong and influential group of evangelical clergy and laity in the Church of England, well organized, which opposes any approach to organic union with Rome on grounds of scripture, theology and history. It is in some ways the same group as that which opposed the Anglican-Methodist Scheme on evangelical principles, though there may have been certain modifications in its theology since then. No one needs to be reminded how skilful and effective the opposition of that group may turn out to be. Even more serious, but not yet manifest, is the ingrained anti-Romanism of a large section of the English population, including many of its churchgoers. The cry of 'No Popery' is not often heard nowadays except in Protestant Ulster, but the sentiment which the slogan expresses is very far from dead; it is not yet uttered widely, because the knowledge of a possible union with Rome is not yet widely spread; but a kind of time-bomb may be ticking away.

The issue of 'women priests' will not go away. Many churches of the Anglican communion ordain women, and others will do so soon. The Church of England in due course will no doubt follow suit, for those who believe that the ordination of women is prescribed by the gospel are not likely to be deterred from pressing their case by the embarrassment which could be caused to

Anglican-Roman relations – especially as several Anglican churches ordain women already. If the time comes for Anglican Orders to be fully recognized by Rome, there is no way in which women in priestly orders can be excluded. But the present Pope has proclaimed, and repeated, that the Roman Catholic Church will not ordain women. This difficulty cannot be burked; and no way round it or through it has yet been propounded.[17]

Then there are the non-theological (or rather, non-religious) factors – social, political and psychological – which helped to thwart the Anglican-Methodist Scheme and the Covenanting Proposals, and have confused the international relationships of the Church of England. These surely will operate here also when organic union with Rome becomes a serious possibility (with the interesting variation that Anglicans have feelings of inferiority rather than superiority when they deal with Roman Catholics), though doubtless in greater or lesser strength among different groups than on previous occasions. They are capable of producing a powerful inertia.

These obstacles may be overcome. If so, the 'certain danger' referred to above remains, and it is this: when practical proposals begin to appear which seem able to gain wide approval, many Anglicans, especially those to whom the face of Rome is more acceptable than that of the Free Churches, may well throw themselves so wholeheartedly into bringing final success that they will forget their Christian neighbours, colleagues, partners, brothers and sisters in other churches, and give up all real intention of visible unity with them. They could thus finally divide the churches of this country into two, not exactly hostile, but certainly competitive camps. In some Anglican circles already the word 'ecumenical' refers only to Anglican-Roman Catholic relations – which is of course unhistorical, and more than a little discourteous to those of many churches and nations who initiated the Ecumenical Movement, and sustained it for fifty years before the Roman Catholic Church felt able to take part in it. But, much more seriously, if English Christians are led into a final separation of 'Catholics' and 'Protestants', they will participate not in the consummation of unity, but in its demise.

But this danger can be averted. Unknown to most Anglicans, and perhaps to most Roman Catholics too, conversations have been going on for several years between Methodists and Roman Catholics and between Lutherans and Roman Catholics, both on an international scale and on a national scale; other bilateral conversations involving Rome are also in train. The reports of these conversations show an astonishing similarity at important points – for instance about the nature of the eucharist and of the ministry – to the ARCIC reports, though they have been conducted in entire independence of them.[18] This convergence surely points to the need for the growth of a real relationship between the various bilateral conversations; and in due course to the bringing together of them all. Certain differences will of course remain – to be reconciled, please God, in the future – but the process could well lead towards that fuller unity of all Christian people in this country which has never ceased, in spite of all appearances, to be the real goal of the Church of England, and which is referred to in the conclusion of the ARCIC Final Report: 'It is our hope to carry with us in the substance of our agreement not only Roman Catholics and Anglicans, but all Christians; and that what we have done may contribute to the visible unity of all the people of God as well as the reconciliation of our two churches.[19] And one particularly powerful additional instrument to this end, already to hand, will certainly be *Baptism, Eucharist and Ministry*, the Lima document of the World Council of Churches, the fruit of many years' international and interconfessional study going far beyond the confines of the Anglican and Roman Catholic Churches. This document is already being studied, with appreciation not unmixed with criticism, at many levels of church life by all the English denominations.

6

Doctrinal Pluralism

Before the General Synod of the Church of England finally agreed to take part in the proceedings of the Churches Council for Covenanting, it passed a resolution that enquiry be made into the orthodoxy of the other churches expected to take part, and thus into the eligibility for sharing in a covenant with the Church of England. It was soon judged that the Methodist Church had proved its worthiness at the time of the Anglican-Methodist Scheme; and the other churches – the United Reformed Church, the Churches of Christ and the Moravian Church – were able to pass the test imposed without difficulty. So the Church of England did take part in the work of the Council.

Doubtless this was seen as a necessary preliminary to the covenanting process, but non-Anglicans, when they were reading about this, could not always refrain from a sardonic smile. What, after all, entitled the Church of England to act as the arbiter of orthodoxy? Its own perfect orthodoxy? That is not very evident, and the discreet silence of the bishops, the guardians of Anglican doctrine, amid the welter of conflicting views put forward by Anglican theologians and champions, leaves grave doubt in the mind as to what orthodoxy for Anglicans actually is.

Probably the nervousness of some Anglicans about the doctrinal soundness of others was caused by the fact that the Free Churches do not recite the Creeds in public worship as frequently as does the Church of England – though, in fact, the Apostles' Creed is part of the Baptismal Order and the Nicene Creed part of the Eucharistic Order for Methodists. But it can surely be seen that infrequency of verbal repetition does not disprove genuine conviction, any more than frequency guarantees or deepens it.

What, then, is the situation in the Church of England? Attendance at a different parish church, carefully selected on each Sunday, for two or three months, would begin to give some idea of the range of doctrinal differences within the Anglican community of this country. This range extends from a rigid, 'protestant', scriptural fundamentalism to a rigid, 'catholic', traditionalist fundamentalism. In between are the milder forms of conservative evangelicalism and the milder forms of Anglo-Catholicism; here are also to be found the 'liberals', who have accepted the findings of the older biblical criticism and sit loose to creeds of any kind; the moralists, who interpret the faith chiefly in terms of personal piety and irreproachable behaviour; the radicals, for whom theology is worked out not in conceptual terms but in the pursuit and practice of peace, justice and liberation. In between also are the clergy and laypeople who belong to no party, keep abreast of biblical and historical studies, are open to the views of 'catholics', 'evangelicals', and others, but refuse to regard any set of particular doctrines as exclusive of the others, and seek to integrate the insights which they contain into a truly catholic, ecumenical faith. (Ecumenical Free Church people, who share this faith, thank God especially for this last group, which they know to be large, and with whose members they could easily form one church, if that were ever desirable.)

At the time of the Anglican-Methodist Scheme it was reliably stated that there were seven groups of Anglo-Catholics (all, or nearly all, opposed to the Scheme). The number may have decreased since then, but there is certainly more than one well-organized and articulate group still. Conservative Evangelicals, though they tend to work and vote together, belong to two different traditions. One is descended from John Calvin, accepting and developing his notion of biblical authority and his methods of scriptural exegesis, with residual overtones of predestinationist doctrine and a certain reluctance to place bishops in a different order from that of presbyters. The other stems from those who were influenced by the eighteenth century Evangelical Revival, remained within the Church of England, but retained the 'Methodist' teaching of salvation offered to all, and have not moved very far from the early Evangelical insistence on the verbal inerrancy of scripture. A new element has now come into the picture. There are now the strongly motivated 'charismatics' in the Church of England who in their concern for the gifts (rather than the fruit) of the Holy Spirit adopt a somewhat simplistic attitude to the scriptures, are not greatly interested in the social witness of the church (though they are generous in personal charity), and have little use for dogma or Church Order.

It could at one time be said that for all the doctrinal differences observable in the Church of England, any Anglican, and indeed any other Christian, could be sure that wherever he attended Anglican worship the liturgy would be the same, since the Book of Common Prayer was in use everywhere. And it was argued from this that the church was one in faith, despite all differences, since it was one in liturgy, and liturgy is the most authentic expression of faith. It has no longer been possible to adduce this argument since variations in liturgy were first permitted by way of experiment, and are now authorized in the form of the Alternative Service Book (1980). Indeed, on these lines, since the eucharistic liturgies in the ASB are so very similar to the modern vernacular Mass of the Roman Catholic Church and to the Sunday Service of the Methodists, and so unlike the Order of Holy Communion in the Book of Common Prayer, it could perhaps be argued that the section of the Church of England which mainly uses the ASB is more closely associated with the Roman Catholic and Methodist Churches, than it is with the rest of the Church of England. But this is an over-paradoxical conclusion.

Identity of liturgical pattern and even of words can in fact do no more than point towards a convergence of doctrine; it does not demonstrate or cement organic unity. So in the days when the Book of Common Prayer reigned unchallenged, identity of words and order only served to cloak, and not in any way to reconcile, the huge differences in doctrine between those who believed in some form of transubstantiation and those who were content with a Zwinglian view. Anglicans and non-Anglicans alike were fully aware of this fact. Free Church people attending Anglican worship could easily sense the doctrinal atmosphere, sometimes finding themselves in a world where the bleakness of the ceremonial reminded them of the purely verbal worship which was now outgrown in their own churches, sometimes in an atmosphere of colour and fragrance and elaborate gesture which they had associated with the Church of Rome (whereas they often felt very much at home in the simplicity of modern Roman Catholic worship).

But perhaps it could be objected that we are overstressing the divergences and contradictions in Anglican doctrine as it is held by Anglican teachers. Does not the Declaration of Assent, authorized in 1975, and required frequently, as we have seen,[1] of all clergy from their ordination onwards, indicate a much greater agreement on doctrine than has so far been acknowledged in this chapter? It is necessary at this point to quote the Declaration in full, although part of it has already been given for the purposes of the earlier discussion.[2]

Preface

The Church of England is part of the One, Holy, Catholic and Apostolic Church worshipping the one true God, Father, Son and Holy Spirit. It professes the faith uniquely revealed in the Holy Scriptures and set forth in the catholic creeds, which faith the Church is called upon to proclaim afresh in each generation. Led by the Holy Spirit, it has borne witness to Christian truth in its historic formularies, the Thirty-Nine Articles of Religion, the Book of Common Prayer and the Ordering of Bishops, Priests and Deacons. In the declaration you are about to make will you affirm your loyalty to this inheritance of faith as your inspiration and guidance under God in bringing the grace and truth of Christ to this generation and making him known to those in your care?

Declaration of Assent

I, A.B., do so affirm and accordingly declare my belief in the faith which is revealed in the Holy Scriptures and set forth in the Catholic Creeds and to which the historic formularies of the Church of England bear witness; and in public prayer and the administration of the sacraments, I will use only the forms of service which are authorized or allowed by Canon.

Anyone who knows the tangled and turbulent history[3] of subscription to the Thirty-Nine Articles, first required of Anglican clergy by the Thirty-Sixth Canon of 1604, will sympathize with those who hope that the Declaration of 1975 has brought this history to a happy ending. The Articles were originally imposed as a kind of 'standard' (not quite a 'confession') of sound Anglican doctrine, with a view to the unity and harmony of the Church of England. They avoid the extreme forms of both Roman and Protestant doctrine. Without doubt, both in theory and practice, they are patient of much variety of interpretation, and in this way did much to preserve the unity and harmony which were their aim. In particular, by refraining from precise statements of Anglican doctrine on every controversial matter, they have allowed growth and development within the Church of England. But this very growth and development gradually made it difficult, without compromise of conscience, for many Anglican ordinands and clergy to subscribe to them *ex animo*, that is with the whole heart and mind, perhaps especially in relation to those Articles which treat of Original Sin (IX), Works before Justification (XIII), and Predestination and Election (XVII). Hence the amended formula of subscription authorized in 1865: 'I assent to the Thirty-Nine Articles of Religion and to the Book of Common Prayer and of the ordering of bishops, priest and deacons. I believe the doctrine of the Church of England, as therein set forth, to be agreeable to the Word of God . . .'

This new form of subscription certainly helped. But what was meant by 'assent' to the Articles? Acceptance of each proposition contained in the Articles, or general acceptance of the Articles as a whole? And is 'assent' something less than the subscription *ex animo* required in 1604? These questions provoked long and sophisticated arguments, and were not answered to the satisfaction of all before the new Declaration of 1975 was promulgated.

The 1976 report of the Doctrine Commission (*Christian Believing*), drawn up in close relation to the Declaration of 1975, interprets that Declaration quite certainly *not* to mean that those who declare their assent profess their belief in certain theological statements. It goes on, by means of essays written by individual theologians, to indicate the wide variety of interpretations (some very radical indeed) of 'the faith revealed in scripture and set forth in the Creeds' which are regarded by the Church of England, in the judgment of the Doctrine Commission, as legitimately held by those who are ordained to the priesthood or the episcopate. It claims that all these variations fall within 'a common pattern or method of thinking, varying certainly in emphasis from one case to another but concerned in the last analysis with the same ingredients'; and suggests that the vital requirement for Christians today is '. . . to operate within the pattern – that is to use in whatever way or proportion integrity allows the resources which the Christian community makes available'.[4]

If we take the Declaration and the report together – one of them, of course, obligatory, the other the view of an official Commission with no mandatory role, but acting as a kind of high-powered commentator on the Declaration – we are indeed offered a way of tying together the varied theological views propounded in various sections and by various parties in the Church of England. We may leave on one side the awkwardness of the phrase 'belief in the faith' (an awkwardness due to the shifting significance of both nouns in the history of Christian thought). We do not stop to resolve the ambiguity of the phrase 'the resources which the Christian community makes available': is the 'Christian community' identical with the Church of England (an identification which Anglican theologians cannot always be acquitted of making), or does it mean 'the holy catholic church'? Quite aside from these matters we have to ask 'what *is* the pattern, or method, of theology which is characteristic of Anglican theology?'

So many answers, several of them mutually exclusive, have been and can be given to this question that the existence of this pattern has to be called seriously in question. If it *does* exist, is it the pattern of biblical theology, patristic theology, Calvinistic theology, Caroline theology – or even existentialist theology – or a mixture of all? Until we know this – if we can ever know this – we remain in the dark as to what Anglican theology really is, and what its distinctive characteristics really are.[5] We seem to be driven back to the assertion that the distinctive character of Anglican theology is that it has no distinctive character – and not even a distinctive method. And that would lead us back to what seems to be implied by the first Report of the Doctrine Commission in 1938 (*Doctrine in the Church of England*) that the Church of England holds the catholic faith in varying forms: 'The Anglican Churches have received and hold the faith of Catholic Christendom, but they have exhibited a rich variety in methods both of approach and interpretation.'[6] But this is either arrogant or self-evident – arrogant if it means (which it probably does not) that the only genuine holders of the Catholic faith are the Anglican Churches, self-evident if it means that the Anglican Churches hold the essentials of the Christian faith as it has been received by the Universal Church, which no one could possibly deny. Other churches also claim to hold the faith of Catholic Christendom, but do not feel obliged to assert this unless they are challenged to do so. Both Anglican distinctiveness and the power to hold together the discrepant and contradictory elements in Anglican teaching have fallen by the wayside.

It is perhaps significant that the most recent report of the Doctrine Commission, *Believing in the Church* (1981) does not do much in the way of developing the concept of the 'common pattern or method' of Anglican theology, propounded by its predecessor, though it may be said to have made a start by its analysis and frequent illustration of 'corporate believing'.

It seems, then, that the Declaration of Assent of 1975, combined with later discussions and the comments of the Doctrine Commission, does not mark the consensus, with necessary variations, that was hoped for from it. But perhaps we should do well to leave the comments, the Commission's reports, on one side, and attend simply to the Declaration itself? But as soon as we do this, and find that the clergyman is required to declare his 'belief in the faith which is revealed in the Holy Scriptures and set forth in the Catholic Creeds and to which the historic formularies of the Church of England bear witness', we are reminded that the exact point at issue is the content of the faith here mentioned. It is a safe guess that if each member of a group of Anglican ordinands were asked to set out in full what he took that faith to be, many of the documents produced would be in many respects contradictory to others, while some would simply rehearse the basic doctrines of the Christian faith which are common to all Christian churches.

In recent years a particular doctrine of the Christian faith, usually regarded as basic, has become a special focus of division and disquiet. This sort of thing has happened not infrequently in previous history, and has passed off in the end without causing undue disruption, and this is true not only of the Church of England but of many other churches. Examples easily given are the virgin birth and the nature of the resurrection of Christ. But now it is the doctrine of the incarnation that is at stake. If it were possible to characterize the Church of England by its firm adherence to any one set of clauses in the Creeds, the clauses chosen would be those that refer to the incarnation of the word. In many periods of its history, reaching right into the present, the Church of England has been proud to be called 'The church of the incarnation'; and some of the best work done by Anglican teachers and spiritual writers has been in the field of 'incarnational theology'.

But the publication and popularity of *The Myth of God Incarnate* in 1977, not so much by what the Anglican contributors say on the subject – for they have no official status in the Church of England – as by the welcome that their chapters have received in certain Anglican circles, have shown that there is a considerable body of Anglican opinion which is ready to ask the question posed in the first chapter by Maurice Wiles: 'Religion without Incarnation?', without being committed in advance to the traditional Christian answer.[7]

A non-Anglican, reading the 'Anglican' chapters in the book, is likely to be struck by the fact that Anglicans in general hold themselves required to understand the word 'incarnation' much more 'literally' than other Christians, at least in the English-speaking world. 'Literally' as used here, needs explanation. I can believe the phrases in the Nicene Creed, 'And in one Lord Jesus Christ, the only-begotten Son of God – being of one substance with the Father, by whom all things were made, who for us men and for our salvation came down from heaven, and was incarnate by the Holy Ghost of the Virgin Mary, and was made man', in either of two main ways. Either I can believe that it is a precise and literal account of the nature, and the earthly career, of Jesus Christ – that is, I accept as precise the account of the matter worked out by the theologians of the early church in the terms of the metaphysic which they regarded as true. Or I can believe that it was the best available account of an undoubtedly mysterious and probably ineffable subject available in the fourth century and for a long time after that. If I adopt the first alternative, and then find that the patristic metaphysic is untenable, I am on the horns of a dilemma: I must either irrationally cling to my belief in spite of that fact, or I must abandon it altogether. If I adopt the alternative mode of belief, that of accepting the Creeds as the best available account, I may be a little dismayed by the discrediting of the patristic metaphysic, but I am still at liberty to seek and find another way of expressing my faith, since the faith itself is not destroyed by the destruction of the metaphysic.

The Myth of God Incarnate may be said to have destroyed the patristic metaphysic, though some would hold that it had been destroyed long before, and others that its arguments are not con-clusive. For the Anglican authors and many other Anglicans the destruction involved the downfall of the doctrine, so that Christ-ianity, for them, has to live without the doctrine of the incarnation. For others this consequence by no means follows.

But be that as it may. The matter is very contentious. What is probable is that we have here the seeds of a major controversy between those who believe that the doctrine of the incarnation is the heart and soul of Anglicanism, and those who believe that it would suffer only a slight jolt if the doctrine were dropped. The controversy may be confined to academic circles, or it may spread more widely. Such a controversy will have a profound effect, too, on thinking about the eucharist. For what is the presence of Christ in the eucharist if he is not the Son of God, incarnate, crucified, risen and glorified?

It could be, too, that another shadow of division has appeared over the horizon. English Christians have now become aware of 'other faiths', not just as theoretical constructs in books on the history of religions, but as vigorous realities in the life of their own neighbours. Already the lines are drawn in the Church of England – as in other churches – between those who hold that Jesus Christ is the only Way, insist on the evangelization of non-Christians in the most effective (but not uncharitable) way, and reject the practice of inter-faith services; and those who see the 'cosmic Christ', or at least 'the light that lightens everyone', in all the great religions of the world, insist on the validity of these religions and the important insights into God and the world to be found in them, and replace evangelization by dialogue and mutual understanding.[8] Here also the uniqueness of Christ is thought to be at stake by evangelicals; if so, the matter ceases to be simply one of respect and tolerance towards the visitors in our midst, who have now become our fellow citizens, and becomes one of theological principle.

This whole situation of Anglican disagreement – though not in particular the element in it which has just been mentioned – causes considerable difficulty in all ecumenical relationships. When Roman Catholics converse with Anglicans on a global or national scale, they cannot be sure that those with whom they are speaking represent the mind of the Church of England. When the representatives of the Free Churches have been in negotiations with the Church of England on schemes of unity or covenants, they have naturally wished to know what the position of the Church of England is on this or that matter of importance, and they have been met by a variety of answers, many of them conflicting. For it seems to be characteristic of some of the Anglican parties that each of them claims to represent *the* Anglican position. In Local

Ecumenical Projects, where matters of high doctrine do not often rise to the surface, the Free Church participants are frequently puzzled, and sometimes embarrassed, by arguments between Anglican colleagues which threaten the whole existence of the Project, or by the refusal of one Anglican incumbent in a particular area to take part in the Project, while others join in with enthusiasm. And in the end the root of the disagreement, if it is not purely personal, is usually found to be theological; and even when on the surface is about the application of Canon Law, theology is still the real divider.

Recent events in the General Synod, together with the recurrent effects of the division of the Synod into three houses, have led many Anglicans and their non-Anglican friends to wonder whether the Church of England is capable of uniting with any other church. And the theological conflicts which we have listed go a long way towards enforcing a negative answer.

Now, of course, no one, least of all the members of a church, such as the Methodist Church or the United Reformed Church, which allows considerable freedom of theological speculation within a wide framework, wishes the Church of England to enclose itself within the straitjacket of a rigid dogmatic system. The advantages of comprehensiveness have been pointed out already in this book,[9] and they are considerable. But has comprehensiveness, and the relaxation of discipline which goes with it, been stretched so far that the unity and identity of the Church of England are in danger? If that point has not yet been reached, it cannot be far away. Already persons in episcopal office have threatened resignation if certain changes, for example the ordination of women, or the endorsement of certain schemes of unity, are approved. The notion that the various viewpoints in the Church of England make good the deficiencies of each other has a legitimate place. The Church of England can from this point of view be looked at as a whole, and be seen to express something like the wholeness of the faith; and the eccentrics on the fringe can then be seen not to represent the 'real' Church of England, however loud their protestations. 'Creative tension' between different schools of thought, however far apart, can conduce to the health of the whole body, so long as their members refrain from personal recrimination in their writings, and from political machinations in the corridors of Synod. But we have to ask, and ask again and again until a satisfactory answer is forthcoming, whether these convenient and plausible justifications merely provide a mask for the gradual break-up of what used to be a solid and enduring structure. Probably the answer to this question is not nearly so melodramatic as the way in which it is posed may suggest, but it needs to be given.

What of the future if the situation is not taken in hand, and especially if the Establishment continues much as it is at present? It has been suggested by Ronald Preston[10] that the Church of England is on its way to becoming a 'eucharistic sect', though he thinks that this process is even more likely to be completed if disestablishment is carried out. Certainly there has been a vast increase in concentration on the eucharist during the last half century. It is on changes in the eucharistic liturgy that interest in liturgical reform has been focussed, both by its supporters and by its opponents. Meanwhile the connection between the Church of England and the people of England has been steadily eroded, per-haps partly by the eucharistic revival; for ordinary English people who could attend Mattins or Evensong without any great sense of commitment to Christian belief may be repelled by the announce-ment of the parish communion which seems to involve them so much more. So the Church of England may well be tempted to withdraw (insensibly and invisibly, no doubt) into its eucharistic celebrations, in splendid isolation from the indifferent or hostile world. This attitude has always tended to creep into the life of the smaller churches, though not always in a eucharistic form; it may be creeping into Anglicanism too. Indeed, in view of doctrinal differences, it could be leading to the separate life of a *number* of eucharistic sects, loosely coordinated by an episcopal system and the Establishment. This would be a sad rejection of the profound Anglican conviction that the eucharist is the centre from which Christians go out into the world.

But a proposal for the repair of the entire structure has been brought forward by Stephen Sykes in *The Integrity of Anglicanism*.

He suggests with a wealth of supporting argument that the time has come for the renewed and thorough-going study of systematic theology by Anglicans, with a view to the elucidation and development of a distinctively Anglican theological standpoint.[11] This standpoint he believes to exist already, implicit in the liturgy and Canon Law of the church. But it needs to be made explicit and propounded by Anglican theologians 'in the service of their communion and not as though legislating for it'.[12] He believes moreover that an Anglican 'method' of theologizing exists for this purpose, but has not yet been brought fully into play. He does not suggest that the process which he recommends will be quick or easy, nor that it should stifle independence of thought in the minds and words of those who cannot fully accept the final result, and he does not rule out valuable controversy. But he holds that 'it is only the theological exploration of the significances of [the Anglican] inheritance which will begin to establish Anglicanism on lines significant for the future of the world-wide church – on the grounds of its capacity to submit its inheritance to a searching theological appraisal'.[13]

If the fulfilment of such an enterprise is possible – and only Anglicans can decide this issue, and some of them are no doubt already considering it – it will be in a position to add an entirely new dimension to ecumenical discussion; and even the attempt to carry it out would clarify many issues which are at present obscure to Anglicans and non-Anglicans alike. The suspicion, that may be in some minds, that it would make ecumenical conversation more difficult, since distinctively Anglican tenets would have to be contended for by Anglican representatives, is probably unfounded. It is the experience of ecumenists that the clear enunciation of denominational convictions actually forwards the dialogue, not least by indicating where unexpected identity or similarity of view is to be found and where differences still remain. Vagueness and indeterminacy are of no help at all.

Professor Sykes' proposal is, then, attractive, and certainly creates no ecumenical problems. But it is in essence an Anglican response to an Anglican situation. The rest of us are bound to point out that the Church of England now lives in a wider context, and that what it decides for itself is bound to affect us all; and to affect the church in the whole world. So the proposal does not go far enough. It can best be seen as a move towards 'the common confession of the apostolic faith' which is now one of the objectives of the WCC's Faith and Order Commission. Such a confession is not simply a matter of standing up together to recite the Apostoles' and Nicene Creeds – valuable though this is in its own way; it is the proclamation to the world by worship, teaching, life and mission of the faith that we have received in common from the apostles, and still hold in common today, when all differences of interpretation have been explored and taken into account; it is the unity in diversity and diversity in unity which we seek. The process that can lead towards it was begun in a small way in this country by the Anglican-Methodist Scheme of 1968.[14] It was not continued by the Covenanting Proposals. It needs to be taken up again in concert with other churches throughout the world. It goes without saying that in this matter the Church of England can come to play a leading role.

But this is possible only within a new framework of church relations in England; the next and final chapter attempts the first outline of such a framework.

7

A New Pattern for the Future

The ecumenical scene in this country is confused and depressing. No one, high or low, knows in which direction to suggest a move. Meanwhile the churches up till now engaged in conversation and negotiation with each other are slipping back into preoccupation with their own affairs, partly because much business was left unfinished while the ecumenical discussions went on, and must now be finished; but much more because there seems nothing else to do than to relapse into the comforts and security of the old denominational ways. The only hope on or below the horizon springs from the increase and development of Local Ecumenical Projects, but they occupy only a small part of the landscape, and the churches in general still fail to take them with sufficient seriousness.

There is even a tendency in all or most of the churches for their members, including some with a voice which commands attention, to glorify diversity at the expense of unity, and to view with satisfaction the proliferation of independent sects and house churches, however narrow the outlook of these newly created entities may be.[1] Perhaps we have here an example of the human tendency to make a virtue out of necessity, and to identify what we have not tried hard enough to prevent with the purposes of God.

The only church qualified to take the initiative in leading us out of this impasse is the Church of England. Yet this at present is precisely what it is incapable of doing. It has rejected two schemes of visible unity, each one drawn up with a special eye to Anglican convictions and susceptibilities. It is doing some very hard thinking about its ecclesiology and its processes of decision making, but at present it is hampered at nearly every turn by a constitution which in its elaborate provision of checks and balances seems to be designed, or fated, to postpone indefinitely any major change. It is ambiguous in its doctrine because it tries to embrace the contradictory tenets of its conflicting parties without officially admitting that the contradictions exist.

Something more needs to be said about these doctrinal conflicts. They are serious and important, but they are disruptive and destructive partly because they are to be found in a church which believes itself to be orthodox and inviolate, and to possess the truth in a fullness not granted to others. In such a case each school of thought fights to be regarded as the true spokesman of the church, and sets about winning over the whole church to its own point of view. If it is doubted whether this is the present position of the Church of England, the evidence is to be found not only in the foregoing pages, but in all the debates of the General Synod on relations with other churches.

Now most Christians, in this country as no doubt elsewhere, unquestioningly assume that theological, ethical and liturgical differences within the body of Christian believers are accurately indicated by the different denominations bequeathed to them by history. But this is a solemn pretence. The real differences and similarities in most cases – though not all – cut right across the denominations. As a Methodist I have more in common on some matters with an Anglican, or a Roman Catholic, of a particular way of thinking within their churches, than with some of my fellow-Methodists; and they in their turn with me than with their co-denominationalists. This is one of the ways in which denominationalism is now irrelevant. Of course differences between denominations still remain, for instance in the matter of baptismal doctrine; but they have nothing like the importance conventionally ascribed to them.

The Church of England contains within its ample boundaries all these similarities and even the most extreme of these variations. At present, because of the denominational structure of English Christianity, it is reluctant to admit the fact, except when it is forced to do so; other churches also are inclined to insist on their denominational identity rather than on their inclusiveness. So denominationalism, in spite of its irrelevance, still flourishes, like a clear but misleading signpost in a labyrinth of roads.

Is it not possible that the only means of finding the way forward from where we are is for the Church of England to step down from its pedestal, and sit down with the other churches of this country *as equals*? In this way it would retain its prestige but not its privileges, its influence but not its power. The full, frank and formal acknowledgment of parity with other churches would change the whole ecumenical atmosphere, and progressively liberate all the churches from competitiveness, and from feelings of superiority and inferiority, to carry out together, but in diverse ways, the mission to England in which they are all at present ineffectively engaged. It is agreed that mission and unity belong together. Here is a real way of consummating their union. The theological differences which at present divide denominations from each other, and, much more, within themselves, could then be seen on a larger canvas, no longer defensively, and therefore with a much greater hope of reconciliation and the recovery of a true catholicity.

The first step in this 'climb-down' would no doubt be disestablishment, or so radical a revision of the Establishment that the result of it would not easily be recognized as establishment at all. This would be only the first step, but it would pave the way to giving up deliberately and generously the Church of England's more and more dubious, but sturdily defended, claim to be, in and by itself, 'the church of the nation', and it would make room for the creation of a truly national church, various in its manifestations of theology and liturgy and church government (at least at the lower levels), but one in its diversity while diverse in its unity – the church of the land, with Anglican, Methodist, Reformed, Baptist and Roman Catholic strains (and hopefully an admixture of Pentecostalism, Quakerism and Salvationism), in reality as well as in name.

To this end there would need to be a steady dismantling of the social and psychological structures which embody or continue the 'establishment attitude'. The hierarchical pattern of the Church of England and of its constitution would no doubt come under careful scrutiny, but there would be no question, surely, of the abolition of episcopacy, but rather an impetus towards its re-creation and re-invigoration in a conciliar and much more pastoral form; and the overall episcope of the church thus constituted would no doubt be in the hands of a representative council in which bishops would play a leading role. Several of the Free Churches have already signalled their agreement to such an idea; that agreement would become much more widespread and wholehearted when Free Church people were dealing with a non-privileged church.

Granted that the Church of England abrogated its claims, the Free Churches, in fact, need have no eventual difficulty about union with it. In the case of Roman Catholics the complexity would certainly be greater, in view of the international structure and essence of the Roman Catholic Church. But a new Roman Catholicism is being born in England, with affinities both to the Free Churches and to the Church of England without repudiating its own traditions. It cannot be beyond the bounds of possibility that as a new church of the land begins to emerge, it would be eligible for recognition as one of the Uniat Churches of the Roman Communion, like the Churches of Eastern Christendom which are in communion with Rome but retain their own liturgy and their own Canon Law. The way to such realization of unity would certainly be long and arduous, a matter of decades, or even of centuries, rather than of years. It requires a prolonged effort to reach 'the common confession of the Apostolic Faith'. But the quicker and shorter ways have failed to commend themselves to a large enough number of members of the Church of England; and we have to search for 'a longer way round'. Could this be a text for the Church of England? 'Unless a grain of wheat falls into the earth and dies, it remains alone; but if it dies, it bears much fruit'

(John 12.24). And the emphasis could well be on the word 'alone'.

Notes

1 The Credentials of the Church of England

1. W. Palmer, *A Treatise of the Church of Christ*, Volume I, 1836, pp. 325ff.

2. J. H. Newman's publication of some of Athanasius' works, under the title of *Select Treatises against the Arians*, in 1843–4, marks the beginning of this era.

3. Introduction to B. H. Streeter, *The Primitive Church*, Macmillan 1929, p. vii.

4. For the last two years Kingswood School, John Wesley's greatest educational foundation, has held its annual Founder's Day Service in Bath Abbey, and the Abbey has proved to be a magnificent context for Methodist worship and Methodist singing. John Wesley no doubt rejoices.

5. Yet it is sad that the revisers show themselves quite unaware of the hurt and error caused by sexist language.

6. John A. Newton, *Search for a Saint: Edward King*, Epworth Press 1977.

7. I have avoided the words 'ambiguity' and 'compromise' though they are often used in this connexion, since they are now used almost always in a pejorative sense.

8. Ecumenical statements such as *Baptism, Eucharist and Ministry*, WCC/BCC 1983, are beginning to chart this 'unity in diversity'.

2 Constitutional Anomalies

1. The Declaration is again discussed from another point of view on p. 94f.

2. Under the chairmanship of the Bishop of Derby.

3 The Low Standing of Women

1. This is clearly shown by Sara Maitland in *A Map of the New Country: Women and Christianity*, Routledge 1983, pp. 126ff.

2. It is a strange fact that the Orthodox, for all their wonderful insights into the working of the Holy Spirit, do not see any defect in their thinking on this issue. It may be that their definition of traditon precludes such self-questioning.

3. See Kenneth Woollcombe and Philip Capper, *The Failure of the English Covenant*, BCC 1983, pp. 8, 11f. and 34f., for the important part played by this issue in the deliberations of the Churches' Council for Covenanting – and by implication in the opposition to the Covenant in the Church of England.

4. In *Man, Woman and Priesthood*, ed Peter Moore, SPCK 1978, pp. 22ff. The italics are Mascall's.

5. Ibid., pp. 79ff.

6. Such as Gregory Baum and Hans Küng.

7. *The Community of Women and Men in the Church*, the official report of the Sheffield 1981 Consultation, WCC 1983, pp. 20–3.

8. The Bishop of London, Graham Leonard, in a paper given to the Churches' Council for Covenanting, published in the *Epworth Review*, January 1984, pp. 42–9, asserted that it is the role of women to receive and of men to give. This assertion is so manifestly contrary to universal human experience, in which both men and women both give and receive, that it is difficult to see it as anything other than a temporary aberration.

9. The first woman bishop has recently been appointed in the United Methodist Church of the USA.

10. This is substantiated by the research of Richard A. Norris in an American paper (unfortunately not available in Britain) in *Priesthood & the Maleness of Christ: Trinity & Christology in the Fathers*.

4 The Dilemma of Establishment

1. As by R. H. Preston in *The Testing of the Churches, 1932–82*, ed Rupert E. Davies, Epworth Press 1982, p. 74.

2. *Anglican-Methodist Unity: The Scheme*, SPCK 1968, Part 2, p. 94.

3. It is worth noting that very recently G. R. Dunstan, in *Their Lord and Ours: Approaches to Authority, Community and the Unity of the Church*, ed Mark Santer, SPCK 1982, vigorously defends the Establish-

ment by arguments taken from Hooker and Christopher St German, both of whom wrote in the sixteenth century.

4. As is made plain, in guarded terms, by the Preface.

5. So Mark Santer, Bishop of Kensington, in a lecture given at St James', Piccadilly, March 1983, awaiting publication.

6. The Bishop of Kensington refers in his lecture to the 'corruption of the spirit' which is encouraged by the special status of his church.

7. This fact must surely cause great difficulty if the Church of England comes closer to the Roman Catholic Church, which is international.

8. i.e. a Working Party set up by the Board for Social Responsibility of the General Synod. Report published by Hodder 1982.

9. Peter Cornwell, *Church and Nation*, Blackwell 1983, p. 53.

10. Not so much in numbers as in influence on educational, civic, political, ecumenical and theological life. The Channel Isles are similar.

11. The 1851 figures are analysed in O. Chadwick, *The Victorian Church*, Vol. I, A. & C. Black 1971, pp. 363–9.

12. I do not speak here out of much personal experience (though once when I had taken part in an Anglican Induction Service, it was said to me 'You read the prayers very well – you could almost be an Anglican'), but out of the repeated experiences of my Free Church brothers and sisters.

13. Voltaire, *Lettres Philosophiques*.

14. See *The Act of Settlement 1701*, Report of the Working Party G.S. Misc. 15, published by the Church Information Office. It was drawn up in preparation for the Synod debate of November 1982.

5 *Ecumenical Contradictions*

1. A motion to establish full communion with the Church of South India will shortly come before the Synod.

2. The notion of a covenant for visible unity can be said to have come from the United Reformed Church, in the formation of which a covenant had taken an effective part.

3. This is pointed out by R. H. Preston in *The Testing of the Churches*, pp. 82, 83.

4. See below, pp. 40–49.

5. In *The Testing of the Churches*, pp. 149ff.

6. The Anglican–Roman Catholic International Commission.

7. *The Final Report*, Anglican-Roman Catholic International Commission, SPCK 1981, Preface, pp. 1, 2.

8. Ibid., pp. 6ff.

9. Ibid., pp. 13f.

10. Ibid., p. 32.

11. Ibid., pp. 32ff., cf. p. 53.

12. Ibid., pp. 53ff.

13. Ibid., pp. 14ff.

14. Ibid., p. 36.

15. Ibid., pp. 55–8.

16. Ibid., p. 99.

17. There are some encouraging signs in other bilateral conversations, as is pointed out by Mary Tanner in *Their Lord and Ours*, pp. 59f.

18. See the chapter by Mary Tanner, 'ARCIC in the context of Other Dialogues', in *Their Lord and Ours*, pp. 46–72.

19. *The Final Report*, p. 99.

6 Doctrinal Pluralism

1. See above, p. 26.

2. See above, p. 26.

3. Given in full by Thomas Wright in *Believing in the Church*, Report of the Doctrine Commission of the Church of England, SPCK 1981, pp. 109–34.

4. *Christian Believing*, SPCK 1976, p. 5.

5. This part of *Christian Believing* is severely criticized by Stephen Sykes in *The Integrity of Anglicanism*, Mowbray 1978.

6. See William Temple's Introduction to *Doctrine in the Church of England*, SPCK 1938, p. 25. The book was reissued in 1982 by SPCK, with an additional Introduction by G. W. H. Lampe.

7. See *The Myth of God Incarnate*, ed John Hick, SCM Press 1977.

8. See Myrtle Langley in *The Testing of the Churches*, pp. 138ff.

9. See above, pp. 11–15.

10. In *The Testing of the Churches*, pp. 73f.

11. Stephen Sykes, *The Integrity of Anglicanism*, esp. chs 3–7.

12. Ibid., p. 74.

13. Ibid., p. 85.

14. See the chapter on 'Agreement in Doctrine' in *Anglican-Methodist Unity: The Scheme*, pp. 10–17.

7   *A New Pattern for the Future*

1. There is here no intention to disparage the achievements of the fast-growing Black Churches, whose emergence is perfectly understandable in our racially prejudiced society and among our racially embarrassed churches.

Index

Act of Settlement, 72
Alternative Service Book, 8, 12, 13, 19, 26, 59, 93
Andrews, L., Bishop, 9
Anglican-Methodist Scheme, 12, 21, 23, 30f., 57, 75f., 79, 80ff., 83, 84, 88, 89, 92, 104
Anglo-Catholics, 92
Appeal to all Christian People, 75, 78
ARCIC, 84, 86ff.
Archbishop of Canterbury, 52, 53, 56
Athanasius, St, 3, 110

Balliol College, Oxford, 56
Baker, J. A., Bishop, 78
Baptism, Eucharist and Ministry, 44, 99, 110
Baptists, 24, 36, 65, 67, 70, 108
Barnes, E. W., Bishop, 33
Bath Abbey, 110
Baum, G., 44
Believing in the Church, 97, 113
Bell, G. K. A., Bishop, 75, 77
Berkeley, G., Bishop, 8
Birmingham, 68
Bishops, House of, 25
Black Country, The, 68
Board for Mission and Unity, 28, 34
Book of Common Prayer, 5, 6, 12, 13, 14, 17, 19, 26, 59, 93, 94f.
Bristol, 25, 68
Bristol Handbook to Local Ecumenical Projects, 24
British Council of Churches, 77, 79, 81
Butler, J., Bishop, 8

Callaghan, J., 33
Calvin, J., 92
Cambridge, University of, 11, 53, 55, 64, 86
Canons
—A8, 28
—B9, 20
—B15A, 21ff.
—B132, 20
—C13, 54
—C15, 26ff.
Canon Law, 18ff., 101
Capper, P. N., 111
Cardinal Archbishop of Westminster, 62
Caroline Divines, 3, 8
Catholic Emancipation, 67
Chadwick, O., 112
Channel Islands, 112
Chaplain General, 55
Charismatics, 93
Charles I, 9
Christian Believing, 96, 113
Christian Socialists, 60
Church and Nation, 63
Church and the Bomb, The, 62
Church Assembly, 29
Church Commissioners, 34, 53f.
Churches of Christ, 76, 91
Church Estates Commissioners, 53
Church House, Westminster, 31
Church Times, 85
Churchill, W., 33
Cistercian Abbesses, 49
Clarendon Code, 11

Index

Index

Moorman, J. R. H., 76
Moravian Church, 24, 76
Movement for the Ordination of Women, 36
Myth of God Incarnate, The, 98f.

Newman, J. H., Cardinal, 8, 83, 110
Newton, J. A., 9
Nonconformists, 55, 66, 67
Norris, R. A., 111
North India, Church of, 14, 76, 78

Oath of Allegiance, 54
Old Catholics, 78
Oldham, J. H., 75
Order of Holy Communion, 6
Ordering of Bishops, Priests and Deacons, 94f.
Ordination of Women in Ecumenical Perspective, The, 44
Orthodox, Orthodox Churches, 37, 41, 42, 44f.
Oxford, 35
Oxford, University of, 11, 53, 55, 64, 86

Palmer, W., 110
'Partners in Mission', 70
Paul, St, 47f.
Pentecostalism, 108
Pilgrim's Progress, The, 66
Presbyterians, 22, 36, 65f., 67, 75 (see also United Reformed Church)
Preston, R. H., 102, 111, 112
Priesthood and the Maleness of Christ, 111
Prime Minister, The, 33f., 52
Primitive Church, The, 110
Puritanism, 66

Queen, The, 17, 19, 27, 33, 34, 52, 54, 55, 56, 59
Queen Anne's Bounty, 53

Rahner, K., 59
Ramsey, A. M., Archbishop, 8, 77, 83
Rodger, P. C., Bishop, 77

Roman Catholics, Roman Catholic Church, 2, 4, 15, 24, 37, 44f., 54, 55, 64, 65, 67, 68, 69, 71, 84, 86ff., 93, 94, 100, 106, 107, 108

Royal Marriages, 72
Runcie, R., Archbishop, 45f.

Salvation Army, 108
St German, C., 112
Santer, M., Bishop, 111, 112
Scotland, Church of, 75
Search for a Saint, 110
Shape of the Liturgy, The, 6
Sheffield, 68
Simeon, C., 9
Society of Friends, 36, 108
Soper, Lord, 32, 53
South India, Church of, 14, 70, 75
Stockholm, 75
Streeter, B. H., 4
Sweden, Church of, 78
Sykes, S., 102f., 113
Synod, General, 18, 21, 29f., 53, 62f., 73, 76, 81, 82, 101

Tanner, M., 113
Taylor, J., Bishop, 9
Temple, W., Archbishop, 8, 33, 75, 77
Testing of the Churches, The, 111, 112, 113
Thatcher, M., 33
Their Lord and Ours, 111, 113
Times Educational Supplement, The, 56
Tinsley, J., Bishop, 57
Tomkins, O. S., Bishop, 77
Tractarians, The, 3
Treatise of the Church of Christ, A, 110
Trollope, A., 32

Uniat Churches, 108
Ulster, 88
United Methodist Church of USA, 111
United Reformed Church, 14, 24, 27, 65f., 76, 91, 101, 107